U.S. RESPONSES TO CHINA'S FOREIGN INFLUENCE OPERATIONS

HEARING

BEFORE THE

SUBCOMMITTEE ON ASIA AND THE PACIFIC

OF THE

COMMITTEE ON FOREIGN AFFAIRS
HOUSE OF REPRESENTATIVES

ONE HUNDRED FIFTEENTH CONGRESS

SECOND SESSION

MARCH 21, 2018

Serial No. 115–118

Printed for the use of the Committee on Foreign Affairs

Available via the World Wide Web: http://www.foreignaffairs.house.gov/ or
http://www.gpo.gov/fdsys/

U.S. GOVERNMENT PUBLISHING OFFICE

29–390PDF   WASHINGTON : 2018

For sale by the Superintendent of Documents, U.S. Government Publishing Office
Internet: bookstore.gpo.gov Phone: toll free (866) 512–1800; DC area (202) 512–1800
Fax: (202) 512–2104 Mail: Stop IDCC, Washington, DC 20402–0001

CONTENTS

Page

U.S. RESPONSES TO CHINA'S FOREIGN INFLUENCE OPERATIONS

WEDNESDAY, MARCH 21, 2018

House of Representatives,
Subcommittee on Asia and the Pacific,
Committee on Foreign Affairs,
Washington, DC.

The subcommittee met, pursuant to notice, at 2:00 p.m., in room 2167 Rayburn House Office Building, Hon. Ted Yoho (chairman of the subcommittee) presiding.

Mr. YOHO. The hearing will come to order.

Good afternoon, and thank you for being here today on a snow day. When everything else is closed down you guys chose to be here and I thank you for that.

At the 19th Communist Party Congress in October, Xi Jinping proclaimed a new era when China would realize the Chinese dream of national rejuvenation and move closer to center stage and to make greater contributions to mankind.

Part of the contributions Xi intends to make to mankind is the spread of socialism with Chinese characteristics. I think that's still called communism.

He says it is a new option for other countries and nations who want to speed their development while preserving their independence.

For a time, this Chinese model meant a compromise between Communist leadership and a free market principle. Under Xi Jinping, it has increasingly become a byword for one-man authoritarian rule.

At the close of the National People's Congress just yesterday Xi revisited the themes of his party Congress speech but with some major differences.

This time he spoke having—he spoke, having dissolved his own term limits and sharply militaristic tones, saying, "We are resolved to fight the bloody battle against our enemies."

I want to repeat that because I think that's very strong language and I think it sets a tone of the future of their direction. "We are resolved to fight the bloody battle against our enemies with a strong determination to take our place in the world."

State media has begun referring to him as Mao Zedong's title helmsman and fake elected representatives wept in the audience in a Pyongyang-style display of reverence.

Xi is confirming the free world's greatest fears about what he might attempt to do with China's growing power. This is something we all need to be aware of and I thank the panelists for being here.

To accomplish rejuvenation at home and recast the world order in an authoritarian mold, China, under Xi, is making concerted efforts to attain great power, status, and adopting some great power behaviors along the way.

One of these behaviors is growing and spreading its influence around the world. In some respects, this is normal. The United States is not shy in our global efforts to promote democracy and universal values.

But the foreign influence operations that China employs are different than those undertaken by responsible international stakeholders.

U.S. influence efforts are open and transparent, building soft powers which derives from the pervasiveness and attractiveness of the United States and brings about desired outcomes voluntarily.

In contrast, many of China's influence operations are covert and coercive. They seek to distract, manipulate, suppress, and interfere. They create what the National Endowment for Democracy has named "sharp power"—the ability to coerce certain outcomes rather than induce them voluntarily, like soft power.

Here in the United States and abroad, China's coercive influence operations present threats to media integrity, speech rights, academic independence, and political processes.

There is no shortage of congressional interest in this challenge. Just this week, Representatives Moulton and Stefanik introduced a bill to counter foreign propaganda by requiring greater transparency in media, and Representative Wilson introduced legislation that would require Confucius Institutes to register as foreign agents, and hopefully those members will be here. We invited them.

Other offices are working on similar proposals and broader related reform efforts are underway, including overhauls of the Committee on Foreign Investment in United States and Foreign Agents Registration Act.

Congress is pursuing proactive measures as well such as my own BUILD Act to reform development finance efforts and increase U.S. effectiveness abroad using the policies of the United States Government to help people build their own economies for their benefit, unlike the One Belt, One Road, which goes one way and that's to China.

This afternoon I look forward to the panel's view on what more must be done to counter the coercive influence operations and whether Congress should focus on new initiatives, reforming outdated or insufficient authorities, or simply promoting the enforcement and utilization of measures that have already been passed into law.

The challenge before us is significant—not just a threat to our open society but relevant in a much more and a larger global competition.

After the fall of the Soviet Union, democracy stood unchallenged as the surest path to success.

Now Xi is deliberately challenging the supremacy of democracy around the world with his personal brand of authoritarianism. He is presenting the world with a false dilemma that nations must choose between growth and freedom.

If the developing world believes his lies, Xi may succeed in building an alternative order of subservient strongmen who will meekly go along with China's global ambitions in exchange for patronage in their own spheres of influence.

The stakes in this contest are high and China's influence operations are the tip of the spear.

On a final note, I would also mention that the Members of Congress are well aware that the real threat comes from the Chinese Communist Party, not every citizen of China or every person of a Chinese background.

In Australia, the party has sought to discredit reasonable reactions to its interference by casting them as McCarthyist hysterics and making accusations of racism.

I am sure that the same tactics will be deployed as the United States seeks to protect itself from the same coercive influence. Many policy experts have wise warned about the dangers of allowing a rational response to devolve into a reactionary panic.

We will not allow that to happen here.

[The prepared statement of Mr. Yoho follows:]

<u>**U.S. Responses to China's Foreign Influence Operations**</u>
Subcommittee on Asia and the Pacific
House Committee on Foreign Affairs
Wednesday, Mach 21, 2018
Opening Statement of Chairman Ted Yoho

At the 19th Communist Party Congress in October, Xi Jinping proclaimed a new era, when China would "realize the Chinese Dream of national rejuvenation" and move "closer to center stage" to make "greater contributions to mankind."

Part of the contribution Xi intends to make to mankind is the spread of socialism with Chinese characteristics. He says it is "a new option for other countries and nations who want to speed up their development while preserving their independence." For a time, this Chinese model meant a compromise between Communist leadership and free market principles. Under Xi Jinping, it has increasingly become a byword for one-man authoritarian rule.

At the closing of the National Peoples' Congress just yesterday, Xi revisited the themes of his Party Congress speech, but with some major differences. This time, he spoke having dissolved his own term limits, in sharply militaristic tones, saying "[w]e are resolved to fight the bloody battle against our enemies ... with a strong determination to take our place in the world." State media have begun referring to him with Mao Zedong's title "helmsman," and fake elected representatives wept in the audience in Pyongyang-style displays of reverence.

Xi is confirming the free world's greatest fears about what he might attempt to do with China's growing power. To accomplish rejuvenation at home and recast the world order in an authoritarian mold, China under Xi is making concerted efforts to attain great power status, and adopting some great power behaviors along the way. One of these behaviors is growing and spreading its influence around the world. In some respects, this is normal. The United States is not shy in our global efforts to promote democracy and universal values.

But the foreign influence operations that China employs are different than those undertaken by responsible international stakeholders. U.S. influence efforts are open and transparent, building soft power, which derives from the persuasiveness and attractiveness of the United States and brings about desired outcomes voluntarily.

In contrast, many of China's influence operations are covert and coercive. They seek to distract, manipulate, suppress, and interfere. They create what the National Endowment for Democracy has named "sharp power" – the ability to coerce certain outcomes, rather than induce them voluntarily like soft power. Here in the United States and abroad, China's coercive influence operations present threats to media integrity, speech rights, academic independence, and political processes.

There is no shortage of Congressional interest in this challenge. Just this week, Representatives Moulton and Stefanik introduced a bill to counter foreign propaganda by requiring greater transparency in media, and Representative Wilson introduced legislation that would require Confucius Institutes to register as foreign agents. Other offices are working on similar proposals, and broader related reform efforts are underway, including overhauls of the Committee on Foreign Investment in the United States and the Foreign Agents Registration Act. Congress is pursuing proactive measures as well, such as my own BUILD Act to reform development finance efforts and increase U.S. effectiveness abroad.

This afternoon, I look forward to the panel's views on what more must be done to counter coercive influence operations, and whether Congress should focus on new initiatives, reforming outdated or insufficient authorities, or simply promoting the enforcement and utilization of measures that have already been passed into law.

The challenge before us is significant, not just a threat to our open society, but relevant in a much larger global competition. After the fall of the Soviet Union, democracy stood unchallenged as the surest path to success. Now, Xi is deliberately challenging the supremacy of democracy around the world with his personal brand of authoritarianism. He is presenting the world with a false dilemma—that nations must choose between growth and freedom.

If the developing world believes his lies, Xi may succeed in building an alternative order of subservient strongmen who will meekly go along with China's global ambitions in exchange for patronage and their own spheres of influence. The stakes in this contest are high, and China's influence operations are the tip of the spear.

On a final note, I would also mention that Members of Congress are well aware that the real threat comes from the Chinese Communist Party, not every citizen of China or every person of a Chinese background. In Australia, the Party has sought to discredit reasonable reactions to its interference by casting them as McCarthyist hysterics, and making unsubtle accusations of racism. I'm sure the same tactics will be deployed as the United States seeks to protect itself from the same coercive influence. Many policy experts have wisely warned about the dangers of allowing a rational response to devolve into a reactionary panic. We will not allow that to happen here.

Mr. YOHO. With that, members present will be permitted to submit written statements to be included in the official hearing record and without objections the hearing record will remain open for 5 calendar days to allow statements, questions, and extraneous materials for the record subject to length limitations in the rules, and the witnesses' written statements will be entered into the hearing.

I thank the witnesses for being here today and I now turn to our ranking member from California, Mr. Sherman, for any remarks he may have.

Mr. SHERMAN. Mr. Chairman, you quoted the Chinese leader as demanding for China a place in the world. That is so reminiscent of the demands of Kaiser Wilhelm who demanded for Germany a place in the sun.

Both Germany, slightly over 100 years ago and China today are revisionist powers. We often talk about the lessons of the 1930s and Munich, et cetera. But we would be well advised to study the lessons and the failures of 1914 as we deal with this revisionist power on the other side of the Pacific.

I will have to be absent for part of this hearing because the Middle East Subcommittee is meeting about the Saudi 123 nuclear cooperation agreement, and as a former chair of the Terrorism and Nonproliferation Subcommittee, I will impress them with a few nuggets of alleged wisdom and then return to this room by way of the Financial Services Committee, which is voting at the same time.

China has much to add to the world conversation. A free and fair exchange of ideas is quite reasonable. As a kid, I listened to the short-wave radio from Moscow and Beijing.

We have nothing to fear from the fair presentation of China's views. But when they exercise unfairly acquired economic muscle, an economic muscle acquired through policies that we allow and that Wall Street protects, when they use that economic muscle to snuff out competing voices, then we should be concerned.

I represent more of the entertainment industry than any of my colleagues and we are so proud that we in southern California shape the world's dreams and the world's thoughts.

But there are those who think they should be shaped in Beijing to promote China's preferred narratives. China is trying to take the censorship they've long forced upon their own people and export it here.

And they have two ways to do this. They have the studios by the quotas and they've got the studios by the screens. We have allowed China to send in as many different garments into our country as they choose—big shoes, small shoes, big ties, small ties. We are only allowed to send 35 movies into China.

Now, how does that hurt us? First, it hurts us economically. Second, it means we have a limited impact on Chinese citizens.

But third, it is a statement to every studio in America—if you make a movie we don't like, we won't let it into our country and we won't let in any of your other movies either. We are only going to let in 35.

We could let in the 35 from your competitors. We have got you by the quotas, and whether that quota is 35 or 40, it is critical to our national security that there be no quota at all, and until and

as long as there is a quota, there should only be 35 different garments coming from China into the United States or maybe 17 garments and 18 electronic devices.

Second, we have allowed the AMC Theaters to be acquired by
Chinese interests. So they've got them by the screens. If you make
a movie about Tibet, they are not going to show it on their screens
and they may not show any of your movies on their screens.

That kind of economic power used to cut off the next Tibet movie,
used to demand that never is the Chinese Government or its
agents a villain in any movie. That interferes with free expression
in the United States.

When artists speak out against China on issues of human rights,
they may be blacklisted by the studios or worried about being
blacklisted and kept off either the screens in China or the AMC
screens here in the United States.

And so we see PLA soldiers as heroes in major American movies.
Will we ever see another movie about Tibet?

At the time when China in every international forum talks about
noninterference, China is systematically seeking to control the discussion of ideas here in the United States. This has got to be
stopped and the first step, I believe, are these hearings to shine a
light on it.

But unless we are willing to say no more garments, electronics,
et cetera, can come into our country under terms that are different
than our movies can go into their country, they will have us by the
studios.

I yield back.

Mr. YOHO. Well, well said.

Ms. Titus, do you have some opening statements?

Ms. TITUS. Just briefly, Mr. Chairman.

Mr. YOHO. Yes, ma'am.

Ms. TITUS. Well, thank you very much and thank you for holding
this hearing.

You know, as we scale back our diplomatic efforts, we know that
China is ready to step in and fill that power vacuum. It's increasing its influence everywhere.

I serve as a member also on the House Democracy Partnership
and we visit and try to support developing democracies.

Everywhere we go, whether it's Southeast Asia or Latin America
we hear how the Chinese are there, ready to build hospitals, air-
ports, bridges, whatever, and as we pull back they pull in.

I've read some of the testimony and I see that there is a lot of
emphasis in here about transparency, accountability, free exchanges of ideas all being so important in order for us to counter
this censorship that China is pushing.

You also say that actions that fan xenophobia and restrict pluralism just play into their hands. They weaken our democratic institutions and they make the Communist Party's own case for why
we are a flawed system.

I hope that as you proceed to testify or answer questions you'll
address how, under this administration, which seems to exemplify
all of those problems—lack of transparency, lack of accountability,
no free exchange of ideas, xenophobia, build a wall, Muslim ban—

how that kind of politics and rhetoric are hurting our efforts to counter this influence by China.

Thank you, and I yield back.

Mr. YOHO. Thank you for your comments.

Next, we will introduce our panelists.

Mr. Peter Mattis, fellow in the China Program at the Jamestown Foundation; Ms. Shanthi Kalathil, director of the International Forum for Democratic Studies at the National Endowment for Democracy; Dr. Aynne Kokas, assistant professor of media studies at the University of Virginia and fellow at the Kissinger Institute on China and the United States at the Wilson Center.

Thank you for being here. Mr. Mattis, if you'd start.

STATEMENT OF MR. PETER MATTIS, FELLOW, CHINA PROGRAM, THE JAMESTOWN FOUNDATION

Mr. MATTIS. Thank you very much, Mr. Chairman, and for the other members for inviting me to attend. It's an honor to appear before you today.

I've divided my testimony into a few quick parts. The first is why the CCP interferes in countries abroad, a brief description of what they are trying to do, and perhaps I'll spend most of my time focusing on some of our responses.

First is that the Chinese Communist Party places its highest priority on building and maintaining political power and that is not something that is just at home but it is something that in the 20th century communism has always had to push beyond borders because security for these kinds of governments comes from the inside out and there is no obvious sense of where the borders start or where they end.

And if this sounds a little bit abstract, let me read a small section from China's national security law. It says, "National security refers to the relative absence of international or domestic threats to the state's power to govern, sovereignty, unity and territorial integrity, the welfare of the people, sustainable economic and social development, and other major national interests, and the ability to ensure a continued state of security.

National security efforts shall adhere to a comprehensive understanding of national security. Make the security of the people their goal, political security their basis, and economic security their foundation. Make military, cultural, and Social Security their safeguard."

This definition of security has two notable features. The first is that it's defined by absence of threats, not by the ability of the party state to respond to them or to manage them.

This view of security pushes them toward a preemptive approach to thinking about how to cut these threats off before they are ever an issue.

The second is that security extends to the realm of ideas. Some of these dangerous ideas, as they've been identified in CCP documents, include civil society, Western concepts of journalism, and Western concepts of constitutional democracy.

And the combination of these themes—ideas and preemption—almost necessitate the CCP to be looking to shape and interfere with decision making abroad.

And in case we think that this is something that is sort of a rogue actor or it's just one agency here or there or it's not a coherent effort, this is something that is controlled at the highest levels of government, beginning with the Politburo Standing Committee.

There is a member with the responsibility for United Front work on the Politburo Standing Committee who currently is Wang Yang, the chairman of the Chinese People's Political Consultative Conference, and there are Politburo members responsible for the propaganda in the United Front departments.

And it runs all the way through the system. They attempt to do this by shaping the context, the way in which China is discussed, the questions that we ask, and the way we try to frame them—drive the conversation toward perhaps how do we avoid war away from something like how do we compete effectively.

They spend a great deal of effort on controlling the diaspora and that occurs through trying to take over Chinese language media, which is now basically worldwide, is more or less controlled by the CCP, and to a smaller extent, a small group of outlets run by the Falun Gong that can't be squeezed by the party. But most independent outlets have gone away.

There is surveillance on the Chinese diaspora. There is intimidation. There are efforts to mobilize them for political purposes and there is a broad effort to attack or to influence the political core of democracies, and they do this by trying to influence the people with whom you interact, whether it's Americans who speak to you about China or whether it's the people that you meet if you take a trip to China.

They do this by creating high-level dialogues—the Track 2 and Track 1.5—so that they can avoid the filtering that staff or other professionals who are focused on China might provide, and counter intelligence officials in the United States, in Canada, in Australia, in New Zealand as well as others have seen efforts to try to build up local politicians because today's councilman might be tomorrow's legislator at the national level.

In terms of a response, it's not that we don't necessarily have the law or the tools. It's that there has to be the prioritization coming from the top and for the executive departments that are most responsible like the Department of Justice.

At the next level you need a higher level of knowledge than we have of Chinese activities and how the Chinese Communist Party functions, and we also need to keep the discussion open and not let it be shut down, because ultimately we are a democracy. We do allow freedom of speech. We do allow freedom of association and expression.

And the public conversation is important because the government resources will only ever be focused on the illegal rather than sort of the gray area and it's up to us as citizens to decide what is okay—what is appropriate engagement.

[The prepared statement of Mr. Mattis follows:]

"U.S. Responses to China's Foreign Influence Operations"
Testimony before the House Committee on Foreign Affairs, Subcommittee on Asia and the Pacific - March 21, 2018
Peter Mattis
Fellow, The Jamestown Foundation

***

Thank you for the opportunity to present my testimony here today. It is an honor and a privilege to appear before the committee.

I've organized my testimony into several parts, explaining why the CCP interferes in other countries' domestic politics, some of the party's activities inside the United States, and what the U.S. Government can do to counter harmful CCP interference and influence.

The Chinese Communist Party Shapes the World

The Chinese Communist Party (CCP) places its highest priority on building and maintaining its political power. As a Leninist party, it organizes the political world around a revolutionary vanguard formed of professional political operatives. This political core attempts to govern and shape society through social organizations — e.g. trade unions, writers' guilds, etc. — or installing party committees to oversee the management of other organizations outside the direct control of the party. Communism since the 19th Century always has had an international dimension, because there is no obvious border for where a party like the CCP should stop. The most important threats that must be addressed are the diaspora communities and potentially threatening great powers. The former have the cultural knowledge to introduce subversive ideas that resonate. The latter have the material power to undermine or topple the party-state.

In case this sounds too abstract, the desire to control the political landscape and protect the party's position found clear, contemporary definition in China's National Security Law (2015). The law describes security in broad, encompassing terms that goes well beyond physical threats to the territory of the People's Republic of China. Security comes from the inside out. Articles Two and Three of the law state:

> "National security refers to the relative absence of international or domestic threats to the state's power to govern, sovereignty, unity and territorial integrity, the welfare of the people, sustainable economic and social development, and other major national interests, and the ability to ensure a continued state of security. National security efforts shall adhere to a

comprehensive understanding of national security, make the security of the
People their goal, political security their basis and economic security their
foundation; make military, cultural and social security their safeguard..."
This definition has two notable features. First, security is defined by the absence of threats,
not by the ability to manage them. This unlimited view pushes the CCP toward pre-empting
threats and preventing their emergence. Second, security issues extend to the domain of
ideas. What people think is potentially dangerous. The combination of these themes —
preemption in the world of ideas — creates an imperative for the party to alter the

One way of making this concrete is to look at some of the CCP documents about security
threats. In April 2013, the CCP circulated "Document No. 9" — officially titled
"Communiqué on the Current State of the Ideological Sphere" — that identified some of the
ideas that undermined the party-state's security. Among these ideas were the promotion of
constitutional democracy, civil society, and Western concepts of journalism. In the circular's
final paragraph, it stated the party should "allow absolutely no opportunity or outlets for
incorrect thinking or viewpoints to spread." Influencing the outside world, therefore, is not
just a historical activity of the party, but a requirement for national security.

The CCP documents and media identify several areas of activity that Americans would
describe as influence operations or fall under the framework of covert action. Principal
among these activities are united front work and external propaganda work. They have a
long history within the CCP, dating to the Chinese Revolution and the Civil War that
followed World War II.

The most important of these activities is called united front work. United front work has a
Leninist heritage and was imported from the CCP's Soviet counterparts. Mao Zedong's pithy
description of united front work continues to resonate in the party's publications: "to
mobilize [the party's] friends to strike at [the party's] enemies." Mao described united front
work as a kind of "magic weapon" on par with the military power of the Red Army (the
Revolutionary Era name for the People's Liberation Army). The purpose of united front
work is to build politically-useful coalitions or social organizations and mobilize them for
political action. United front publications and Xi Jinping's speeches identify supporting great
rejuvenation of the Chinese people, safeguarding the party-state's core interests, and
pursuing national unification as the key objectives of united front work.

The second most important is propaganda work, which like united front work, has both
internal and external dimensions. The CCP's external propaganda is delivered through a
variety of means, including media networks at home and abroad, spokespeople, academics,
and nearly any other venue that can conceived to broadcast information. Developing

international "discourse power" has been a party priority for at least the last decade, and Beijing has invested billions of dollars into giving its propaganda outlets global reach.

CCP Institutions of Influence Operations

The CCP's organization of influence operations flows down from the Politburo Standing Committee to the grassroots levels of the party. This is not an area in which we can say the CCP leadership does not know or that rogue actors are driving policy. United front and propaganda work have been and continue to be key elements of the party's day-to-day operations. Three layers exist in this system, including the responsible CCP officials, the executive/implementing agencies, and supporting agencies that

On the first level, several CCP officials oversee the party organizations responsible for influence operations. They sit on the Politburo Standing Committee (PBSC) and the Politburo. The senior-most united front official is the Chinese People's Political Consultative Conference (CPPCC) chairman, who is the fourth-ranking PBSC member. The other two are the Politburo members who direct the United Front Work Department (UFWD) and the Propaganda Department. These two often sit on the CCP Secretariat, which is empowered to make day-to-day decisions for the routine functioning of the party-state. Even a brief thumbnail sketch of the current officeholders shows that these are individuals who have proven themselves in party positions at every level, and, while some maybe Xi Jinping loyalists, they are basically competent officials who should be taken seriously. The current holders of these positions are the following:

- CPPCC Chairman Wang Yang: Wang is former vice premier and party secretary of Guangdong Province and Chongqing. He rose through the party ranks in Anhui Province, and he served as State Council deputy secretary and National Development and Planning Commission vice minister.
- UFWD Director You Quan: You is the former party secretary of Fujian and served for two decades in progressively more senior staff positions in the State Council General Office.
- Propaganda Department Director Huang Kunming: Huang moved up the party ranks, before taking over Zhejiang Propaganda Department in 2007 in his first position within this system. After a brief stint as Hangzhou Party Secretary in 2012-2013, he became a deputy director in the Propaganda Department.

The second level contains the three party organizations headed by the aforementioned leaders. These are the leading agencies through which the CCP builds political influence and power.

- Chinese People's Political Consultative Conference (CPPCC): The CPPCC, according to the organization's website, is "an organization in the patriotic united front of the Chinese people, an important organ for multiparty cooperation and political consultation." The advisory body mediates between important socials groups and the party apparatus. The CPPCC is the place where all the relevant united front actors inside and outside the party come together: party elders, intelligence officers, diplomats, propagandists, military officers and political commissars, united front workers, academics, and businesspeople. They are gathered to receive instruction in the proper propaganda lines and ways to characterize Beijing's policies to both domestic and foreign audiences. Many of these individuals, particularly if they hold government positions, are known for their people handling skills and have reputations for being smooth operators. CPPCC membership offers access to political circles and minor perquisites like expedited immigration. The CPPCC standing committee includes twenty or so vice chairpeople who have a protocol rank approximately the same level of a provincial party secretary. At the central level, the CPPCC includes more than 2,200 members, but the provincial and local levels include another 615,000.
- United Front Work Department (UFWD): The UFWD is the executive agency for united front work. It has a variety of responsibilities at home and abroad, including in the following areas: Hong Kong, Macao, and Taiwan affairs; ethnic and religious affairs; domestic and external propaganda; entrepreneurs and non-party personages; intellectuals; and people-to-people exchanges. The department also takes the lead in establishing party committees in Chinese and now foreign businesses. The UFWD operates at all levels of the party system from the center to the grassroots, and the CCP has had a united front department dating to the 1930s.
- Propaganda Department: This department has been a core part of the CCP since 1924. The official description of the Propaganda Department's duties includes the party's theoretical research; guiding public opinion; guiding and coordinating the work of the central news agencies, including Xinhua and the People's Daily; guiding the propaganda and cultural systems; and administering the Cyberspace Administration of China and the State Administration of Press, Publication, Radio, Film, and Television.

The Overseas Chinese Affairs Office (OCAO) does not fit easily into this framework. The office's leadership is not as senior as those of the UFWD, Propaganda Department, and the CPPCC, but it plays an important role in the CCP's efforts to leverage Chinese abroad. The OCAO is routinely involved Chinese communities overseas, and, from its central to local levels, it brings community leaders, media figures, and researchers back to China for meetings and conferences. The official description includes several points relevant to the discussion here: "to enhance unity and friendship in overseas Chinese communities; to maintain contact with and support overseas Chinese media and Chinese language schools; [and] to increase cooperation and exchanges between overseas Chinese and China - related to the economy, science, culture and education."

On the third level, many other party-state organizations contribute the party's influence operations. Their focus is not on united front or propaganda work, but they still have capabilities and responsibilities that can be used for these purposes. Many of these agencies share cover or front organizations when they are involved in influence operations, and such platforms are sometimes lent to other agencies when appropriate.

- Ministry of State Security
- Ministry of Foreign Affairs
- Ministry of Culture
- Ministry of Education
- State Administration for Foreign Expert Affairs
- Ministry of Civil Affairs
- Xinhua News Agency
- Liaison Bureau of the People's Liberation Army Political Work Department

Operations Affecting the United States

There are a number of different ways to categorize what Beijing is doing in the United States. I have chosen three areas — shaping the context, controlling the Chinese diaspora, and targeting the political core — to describe some of the main lines of effort of CCP united front and external propaganda activities.

Shaping the Context: The CCP spends a great deal of effort on seemingly softer measures to shape the context through which China is understood. These activities were described by American China scholar Perry Link as the "anaconda in the chandelier," which encourages self-censorship rather than upsetting the snake lurking above. Self-regulating behaviors are difficult to identify and prove the party's actions as the root cause

- Selective Visa Approvals: Everyone in the China studies field is aware that they must be careful with what they say and what they write if they wish to maintain access to China. Twenty or more years ago, visa denials were relatively rare and the few people blacklisted were well-known. Now, the younger and younger scholars and analysts have visa troubles, and the general frustration of dealing with what is sometimes a capricious visa process makes it difficult to know when one has crossed a red line.

- Manipulation of History and Records: Chinese archives, databases, and Internet materials routinely change form or disappear from the public record. In some cases, these may appear to be age-old policy debates, but may have contemporary resonance because they show the CCP considered options now anathema within the party. The CCP also has applied pressure to Western academic publishers to limit or otherwise tailor access to materials available behind the Great Firewall.
- Academic Programs: CCP programs, like the Confucius Institutes, are less important for their specific content in dealing with U.S. universities than for establishing a relationship. By facilitating U.S. universities investment in facilities, research collaboration, or programs, the CCP creates a vulnerable relationship that can be used to apply pressure to the university unless the latter is prepared to walk away.

Controlling the Chinese Diaspora: The CCP attempts to mobilize Chinese society at home and abroad by incentivizing cooperation, discouraging neutrality, and coercing compliance. Part of the point of this effort is to reflect the CCP's power and authority back into China for PRC citizens. This reflection highlights the strength of the party and the absence of an international challenge to its legitimacy and authority.

- Buying Up Chinese-Language Media: Over the last 15 years, the CCP steadily chipped away at independent Chinese-language media overseas. Media control was built up through outright purchases of existing media organizations, purchase by proxy, or driving independent newspapers bankrupt by organizing advertiser boycotts. Today, the largest non-CCP media in the Chinese language are all associated with the Falungong. Overseas Chinese media owners and publishers regularly attend conferences back in China where they can be told the current and upcoming propaganda lines.
- Surveillance and Intimidation: The CCP monitors the Chinese diaspora quite closely in order to apply pressure where appropriate. Some of this intimidation is quite invasive, including threats to and arrests of family members back in China. PRC Government officials and journalists attempt to track individuals who attend politically-sensitive events and who shows up for pro-PRC rallies.
- Mobilizing to Support China: The CCP also mobilizes overseas Chinese, regardless of citizenship, to turn out for leadership visits, protests of the Dalai Lama, territorial disputes, or other political events viewed unfavorably by Beijing, and, in the past, the Olympic torch relay. In other cases, community organizations are used to drive letter-writing campaigns to legislators to pressure them in directions favorable to Beijing.

Targeting the Political Core: The CCP targets the political and policy elite from above and below. At the top levels, the CCP engages unwitting naifs and witting co-conspirators to deliver its messages directly to U.S. decisionmakers without filtering through staff. At the lower levels, the CCP through community organizations assists the political careers of sympathetic persons. Local races do not require the same resources for national elections. And today's councilperson is tomorrow's Congressional representative.

- Consultants: The exoticism with which we treat China has given rise to a cottage industry of people interpreting China or leveraging their political connections to open doors for U.S. businesses. These consultants, especially former government officials, are paid by the U.S. business, but Beijing may have directed the company to engage this or that consultant as a way to reward their service. The business gains access to China. The consultant gets paid and then assists the CCP in delivering its reassuring messages to colleagues still serving in government.
- Dialogues: A number of U.S.-China Track 1.5 and Track 2 dialogues are managed by united front organizations on the Chinese side, such as the Sanya Initiative. These meetings offer the access and opportunity to brief U.S. participants on particular messages or themes. The value comes from U.S. participants who are able to relay those messages without staff filtering to senior policymakers. Although Americans often see these dialogues as a way for mutual influence, the united front cadre chosen for these meetings are those the party trusts to operate in an ideologically loose environment but still maintain party discipline. Put another way, these dialogues control access and broadcast information; they are not a channel for influence.
- Building Up Local Politicians: Australian, Canadian, and U.S. counterintelligence officials all have reported seeing CCP efforts to cultivate the careers of local politicians. At this stage, even limited support in the form of election funds or voter turnout can make the difference. This is much cheaper than trying to subvert a sitting national-level politician with established loyalties, and this kind of seeding effort has been seen in espionage.
- Agents of Influence: Americans, both wittingly and unwittingly, become the CCP's agents of influence, carrying the party's message to their American friends in business and politics as well as occasionally in the media limelight. These individuals often are successful in business, possessing gravitas and a reputation for knowing China. In the past, CCP leaders like Zhou Enlai made explicit statements about the need to cultivate these people and their reputations, so they could act as a party constituency on a foreign shore.

In many respects, unraveling the CCP influence/interference networks in the United States is a more difficult challenge than in states like Australia, New Zealand, and our Eastern European partners. The basic strength of U.S. laws and institutions has forced the CCP to operate here with a greater degree of sophistication and further below the surface. There are bans on foreign campaign donations. The Foreign Agent Registration Act forces some people acting on behalf of a foreign government to disclose that they are doing so or risk criminal prosecution. Ethics and lobbying rules also provide sunlight on who and how many such agents engage Congressional members and staff. These rules and their enforcement are not sufficient, and they can be dodged. The act of hiding these activities helps prosecutors by demonstrating intent.

Elsewhere in the world where democratic institutions are weaker or allow direct foreign financing for electoral candidates, Beijing has pushed and found openings. Because there is no illegality, the CCP has nothing to hide. Its agents and proxies have not needed to learn ways to cloak their actions. Consequently, the rest of the world provides relevant information about the methods and tools used.

U.S. allies and partners also are targets for CCP influence operations. Regardless whether their relationship with the United States is a driver in Beijing's activities, the CCP's activities in these countries challenge U.S. interests, security cooperation, and values.
- Japan: The U.S.-Japan alliance is the lynchpin of the U.S. security presence in East Asia. Within the alliance, the U.S. and Japanese bases on Okinawa are critical resources for a wide range of contingencies. Japanese security officials believe the CCP has helped stoke the Okinawan separatist movement in an effort to split the alliance and establish the groundwork for solidifying claims in the East China Sea.
- Australia: Australia's problems reportedly center around two billionaires, Huang Xiangmo and Chau Chak Wing, who insinuated themselves into the country's political landscape. Both men donated substantial amounts of money the major political parties and helped establish a network of loyal apparatchiks within Australian political parties. The extent of this influence already has brought down one Australian senator, Sam Dastyari, and the subsequent election was marred by race-baiting, including the local Chinese consulate.
- Canada: In 2010, Canadian Security Intelligence Service chief Richard Fadden stated publicly that municipal politicians in British Columbia and at least two ministers of the crown in the provinces worked on behalf of a foreign government as "agents of influence." Fadden's comments spoke to a long-term CCP effort cultivate officials who ultimately would work at the political center.
- Taiwan: Taiwan faces the leading edge of the CCP's influence operations. Since the election of the Tsai Ing-wen administration and the near collapse of the Kuomintang, Beijing has stepped its activities, including social media and news manipulation. The CCP also supports at least one small political party that largely agitates against the president. The party's campaign also includes squeezing Taiwanese with business in the PRC, so that they act as Beijing's proxies on the island.

U.S. Responses to CCP Influence Operations

My policy recommendations will be divided into three areas: general issues in which Congress plays a role; resolving unenforced laws; and recommendations for new initiatives.

General Issues: Addressing the challenge of CCP influence operations requires thinking broadly about the problem and how to approach it. Overzealous, generalized responses risk alienating the Chinese-Americans most directly affected on a daily basis. They are the most knowledgeable about what the CCP is doing on American streets. The CCP does focus a large portion of its efforts on Chinese emigres, but that effort does not necessarily lead to cooperation or complicity. Chinese-Americans are our citizens and permanent residents, deserving of equal protection under the law. To tackle the CCP's influence operations, the U.S. Government needs their help, and they need the U.S. Government's.

- Keep the focus on the CCP: We are concerned with the Chinese Communist Party, not the Chinese people. The CCP claims to represent all Chinese people, regardless of citizenship, anywhere, all the time. This is not true. Chinese people living outside of the PRC have chosen lives as American, Australian, Canadian, Malaysian, German, and many other non-PRC citizens and residents. When Chinese people make the choice not to be PRC citizens or made that decision generations ago, then both the party and the U.S. Government should respect that choice.
- Encourage Public Discussion: Congress has incredible powers to convene, to drive the public conversation. The capabilities of the executive branch almost certainly will focus on the illegal, because of the way government functions.. Much of the CCP's influence operations occur in a grey area that is not always illegal. For example, there is nothing illegal about Confucius Institutes or endowing a university chair. What is appropriate and acceptable in dealing with the CCP or its proxies can be discussed, and the rules of engagement only can be sorted out through conversation.
- Raising Costs for CCP Interference: Right now, Beijing faces few if any consequences for its interference inside the United States. Forcing the CCP to introduce additional cutouts and layers of complexity may be temporary fixes, but they do require additional resources and make the party's activities inefficient. When Education officials at the PRC embassy and consulates show up at universities to threaten students or turn them out for a rally, the U.S. Government can revoke their diplomatic status. Travel restrictions can be placed on such officials.

Stepping Up Enforcement: The U.S. Government has many tools for investigating and countering CCP interference in American society. In some cases, pushing back against CCP activities means enforcing the laws already on the books. Using legal tools, however, requires the Department of Justice to an active role. The department needs lawyers who are fighting to say "yes" to pursuing cases rather than looking for reasons to say "no."

- Improving Counterespionage Capabilities: The executive branch has failed to prosecute or botched investigations into Chinese espionage here. This may seem a far cry from the CCP's influence operations. The same parts of the Intelligence Community and the Department of Justice that perform counterespionage, however, are the same parts that will take the lead on countering CCP interference. If they have difficulty prosecuting (relatively-speaking) straightforward Chinese espionage cases, then countering CCP influence is likely to be too complicated. Successful espionage prosecutions, in a sense, are the analytical, investigative, and legal training ground for the capabilities the U.S. Government needs to deploy. The failure to do this well alienates the Chinese-American community, which has reasonable concerns about racisms, and lets those breaking the law in support of CCP interests that the risks are low. Below are just a few examples from recent years of problems, and I have been assured by several knowledgeable officials that many worse examples are not public:
    - Chen Yanping: Dr. Chen is president of the University of Management and Technology (UMT), and the Department of Justice declined to prosecute her on variety of charges after failed plea negotiations. Chen helped found UMT, an online, for-profit university focused on recruiting students in the U.S. military. She is or was a Chinese military officer and CCP member. Much of UMT's student information reportedly was stored on servers in Beijing. The school created a whistle-blower after Chen directed one of the staff to focus on recruiting students from Wright-Patterson Air Force Base, which is an important Air Force intelligence facility.
    - Helen Gao: Helen Gao was a contract translator for the U.S. Department of State between 2010 and 2014, who confessed to providing information on her colleagues and their activities. A person who she believed to be an intelligence officer approached her in China in 2007, asking her to provide information on her social contacts in the United States. She was given a one-time payment of $6,000 at the time and claimed she was wired $5,000 in January 2010. She later lived "briefly for free" with an architect who possessed a top secret clearance for his work designing U.S. embassy facilities for the State Department. That employee admitted to discussing his work on U.S. facilities and his State Department colleagues by name. During her background check for her State Department contract and her U.S. naturalization paperwork, Ms. Gao concealed her relationship with the Chinese intelligence officer. For unknown reasons, U.S. authorities declined to prosecute the case either on charges related to being an unregistered agent or related to lying on immigration and security paperwork.

- ○ Charges were withdrawn in 2015 against National Weather Service hydrologist Sherry Chen and Temple University physics professor Xi Xiaoxing. Both scientists, separately, had contact with Chinese government officials or scientists. Poorly-run investigations led to a rush to judgment and then ultimately a failure to generate any workable charge. Regardless whether it was a failed or misguided prosecution, cases such as these burn the goodwill of the Chinese-American community that has plenty of reasons to doubt impartial enforcement of U.S. law.
- Enforcing the Foreign Agent Registration Act (FARA): The gaping holes in FARA notwithstanding, the law effectively can be wielded to shine a public light on CCP influence operations. The National Security Strategy and the National Defense Strategy provide an explicit statement from the executive branch that U.S. policy toward China has changed. Further clarification and wide promulgation of these changes coming from the White House would close some of the FARA loopholes for those acting on behalf of the CCP who can no longer justify their actions as supporting U.S. engagement of China consistent with policy.
- Leveraging Civil Rights Legislation: "Conspiracy Against Rights" (U.S. Code, Title 18, Section 241) could be used against united front and undercover CCP agents, such as intelligence and security officials, who threaten, coerce, or intimidate Chinese people (or others) in the United States. The provision makes it unlawful for two or more persons to conspire to "injure, oppress, threaten, or intimidate any person in any State, Territory, Commonwealth, Possession, or District in the free exercise or enjoyment of any right or privilege secured to him by the Constitution or laws of the United States, or because of his having so exercised the same." Other related civil rights legislation also could be used if efforts to counter CCP interference qualified as federally-protected activities.

Additional Policy Recommendations: In countering the CCP's influence operations, the U.S. Government needs both forcing events and clear prioritization from the top. Clarity of mission needs to come from the White House and the Department of Justice. Justice, the FBI, and the Intelligence Community all need greater and more distributed understanding of the challenges. Priority and knowledge, however, are two things that cannot be legislated.

- Annual Report to Congress on the CCP's Influence and Propaganda Activities: In the Reagan years, the U.S. Government published an annual report on Soviet active measures. The report forced government agencies to come together to discuss the problem and make decisions about what information needed to be released for public consumption. A similar report on the CCP's activities would have the beneficial effect of raising awareness and convening disparate parts of the U.S. Government that may not often speak with each other. A classified annex could be produced for internal government consumption.

- Boosting FBI Intelligence Collection: The FBI needs additional resources to counter Chinese influence and intelligence operations. Apart from the bureau's administrative problems, its toolkit does not allow agents to operate effectively as intelligence gatherers rather than law enforcement officers. FBI agents need stronger Chinese-language capabilities. Too few agents speak Mandarin, much less any of the common dialects, like Cantonese or Shanghainese, among American Chinatowns. Without language skills, FBI agents cannot collect intelligence effectively or follow leads to map the CCP presence. Analysts and translators perform different tasks and cannot substitute. At least for the FBI's China squads, agents need better cover options. FBI agents and supervisors currently have a choice between using the badge or long-term undercover operations. They need the ability to use other U.S. Government cover or business covers to work the streets.
- Improving FARA and Counterespionage Statutes: Tightening up these statutes to cover "agents of influence" and add teeth to FARA's focus on voluntary compliance would expand the toolkit for law enforcement to crack down. Although one can argue that existing statutes are sufficient, the caution with which they have been enforced suggests a need to tailor the legal language more directly to the problems the United States currently faces.

Mr. YOHO. Thank you for your comments.
Ms. Kalathil.

STATEMENT OF MS. SHANTHI KALATHIL, DIRECTOR, INTERNATIONAL FORUM FOR DEMOCRATIC STUDIES, NATIONAL ENDOWMENT FOR DEMOCRACY

Ms. KALATHIL. Thank you.

Chairman Yoho, Ranking Member Sherman, thank you for the opportunity to testify before the subcommittee on this important issue today.

My remarks will focus on how a rising China has increasingly been able to wield influence that chills free expression within democracies and around the world.

This is not simply about telling China's story, as Chinese authorities like to claim. It is also about shutting down a more contextualized version of China's story and suppressing at a global level the discussion of a growing number of issues that the Chinese Communist Party finds sensitive.

As Xi Jinping's power consolidation and other events have demonstrated, China is moving both in a more authoritarian and a more global direction, which means these trends are likely to intensify.

Over the years within its borders, the Chinese Government has relied on technological innovation to enable advanced censorship and surveillance, which is now made possible by big data and a weak rule of law environment.

Mr. YOHO. I am going to interrupt you a minute. Can you pull that microphone a little closer? We are having a hard time hearing up here.

Ms. KALATHIL. Yes. Is this better?

And control and cooptation of the infrastructure of ideas and communication as key, such that the interests of those powering the infrastructure within China run parallel to, or at the very least, not counter to the interests of the Party.

The CCP has used similar tactics on an international scale to dampen or distort the free exchange of ideas. As noted in the National Endowment for Democracy's recent report on sharp power, authoritarian regimes inevitably project overseas the values that they live by within their borders.

This projection of influence has already had a chilling effect within democracies. Recent examples have been numerous.

Some academic publishers, for instance, have argued that by censoring a small percentage of their content at the source, the remainder can be made available.

Variations of this argument, what you might call the greater good argument, have been advanced by numerous institutions and companies to justify acquiescing to CCP censorship.

Confucius Institutes, which have been lauded internally by Chinese officials as successful influence vehicles, have also come under scrutiny as a growing number of scholars voice concerns that the presence of such Chinese Government-funded centers on campus within democracies including in the United States are constraining academic freedom.

In regions of the world ranging from Latin America to Central Europe to sub-Saharan Africa, the Chinese Government has actively shaped this infrastructure of ideas through backing think tanks, investing in media outlets and infrastructure, and co-opting elites through exchanges and privileged access to officials and experts in China.

Moreover, the Chinese Government's multi-pronged effort to shape the future of the internet has implications for free expression, privacy, and surveillance globally.

Unfortunately, Silicon Valley often invokes the greater good argument to justify its participation in the Chinese Government's censorship or surveillance apparatus.

Why is it important to address this greater good argument, which is advanced by those who say some degree of CCP-imposed censorship or interference is worth tradeoff.

Because in the eyes of the CCP any decision by democracies to compromise their values is binary—either you're willing to do so or you aren't. Degree is unimportant.

For some time, as the CCP's ambitions have grown, democracies have essentially conveyed the message that they are not willing to defend their own core values.

As a result, the Chinese authorities increasingly set the rules with institutions within the democracies on standards of free expression, a development with enormously troubling implications if we remain on this trajectory.

Democracies are slowly coming to grips with this fact. Yet, while the issue must be confronted head on, it would be a mistake to think that the best way to address such heavy-handed tactics by authoritarian regimes is through similarly heavy-handed tactics by democracies that would have the effect of subverting the very values that undergird democratic systems.

Democracies should be proactive in asserting why norms such as transparency, accountability, pluralism, and the free exchange of ideas are critical to their interests.

They must also be precise and thoughtful in formulating nuanced responses to authoritarian influence. Actions that fan xenophobia, restrict pluralism, or contravene core principles will not only weaken democratic institutions but will conveniently make the CCP's own case that democracies are inherently flawed and hypocritical.

With this in mind, democracies might consider several options, including continuing to uncover the ways in which the CCP's influenced activities are impinging on democratic institutions outside China's borders and to share information on best practices for dealing with these activities while respecting democratic values; facilitating democratic learning and supporting the capacity of local independent media to report in a dispassionate way on issues relating to China, particularly in countries and regions without deep capacity to do so; seeking transparency in institutional agreements with Chinese Government-affiliated institutions such as Confucius Institutes and others, collectively supporting existing norms relating to academic freedom and freedom of expression so that individual actors are not susceptible to being picked off and pressured by the Chinese Government or its surrogates; within relevant private sector industries, standing up initiatives that establish voluntary and mutual adherence to accepted norms of free expression and fundamental human rights; and encouraging democratic solidarity among countries that are grappling with their engagement with China.

Such solidarity will invariably lead to more effective and democratically-sustainable outcomes, given the scope of the challenge.

Thank you.

[The prepared statement of Ms. Kalathil follows:]

Statement by Shanthi Kalathil
Director, International Forum for Democratic Studies
National Endowment for Democracy

Before the House Committee on Foreign Affairs
Subcommittee on Asia and the Pacific
Hearing on "U.S. Responses to China's Foreign Influence Operations"
Rayburn House Office Building
March 21, 2018

Chairman Yoho, Ranking Member Sherman, thank you for the opportunity to testify before the subcommittee on this important issue.

My remarks today will focus on how a rising China has increasingly been able to wield influence that chills free expression within democracies around the world. Successfully controlling political speech and expression at home has morphed into a broader approach that seeks to manipulate, suppress and surveil expression and the free exchange of ideas outside China's borders. This is not simply about "telling China's story," as Chinese authorities like to claim – it is also about shutting down a more contextualized version of China's story, as well as suppressing at a global level the discussion of a growing number of issues that the Chinese Communist Party (CCP) finds sensitive.

This has an impact on academic freedom at universities and schools around the world, on the international publishing sector, on communications infrastructure and independent media in developing countries, and on a free and open Internet. Beijing uniquely wields this influence due to China's market appeal and growing stature, employing a combination of carrots and sticks. As Xi Jinping's power consolidation and other events have demonstrated, China is moving in both a more authoritarian and a more global direction – which means these trends are likely to intensify.

<u>Taking domestic tactics overseas</u>

With the advent of the Internet, many originally thought the Chinese government would find it impossible to control the political impact of communication within its borders. But the Internet has not only spread but flourished within China, all while the Chinese government has fine-tuned its management of politically sensitive expression. Since I first began studying this issue many years ago, the shape of the Internet within China has certainly changed, but the overall tactics used by the Chinese government have generally remained stable. First, technological innovation has enabled fine-grained censorship and increasing surveillance, now made possible by tremendous amounts of data collection in a weak rule-of-law environment. Second, while the actual censorship and surveillance apparatus is important, equally important is the inducement of self-censorship at all levels, which relies on fear and an implicit understanding of taboo issues. And finally, control and/or co-optation of the infrastructure of ideas and communication (including the actual pipes, the regulatory environment, and the private sector) is key, such that the interests of those innovating within and powering the information sector within China run parallel to - or, at the very least, not counter to – the interests of the Party.

Just as in the past with respect to the flow of information within China, many now also find it difficult to believe that the CCP can exert influence over expression and communication outside its borders. Yet what we learn from its existing domestic approach is that a) it works; and b) it is possible to use similar tactics on an international scale to dampen or distort the free exchange of ideas. As noted in the National Endowment for Democracy's recent report on "sharp power," authoritarian regimes inevitably project overseas the values they live by within their borders[i]. This projection of influence has already had a chilling effect within democracies.

<u>Impact on democratic principles</u>

Recent examples have been numerous. With respect to encouraging self-censorship, academic publishing in particular has been in the spotlight. Cambridge University Press agreed to Chinese officials' request to censor within China articles pertaining to sensitive issues such as Tibet and the Tiananmen Square massacre; this decision was reversed after protests and petitions from the academic community. Yet publisher Springer Nature went forward with a similar arrangement, arguing that by censoring a small percentage of their content in China, the remainder can be made available. Variations of this argument – the "greater good" argument – have been advanced by numerous institutions and companies to justify acquiescing to CCP censorship.

Confucius Institutes, which have been lauded internally by Chinese officials as successful influence vehicles, have also come under scrutiny as a growing number of scholars voice concerns that the presence of such Chinese government-funded centers on campus within democracies, including in the United States, are constraining academic freedom. This is particularly relevant when the agreements struck between universities and Confucius Institutes are opaque, as they frequently are, and when the educational institutions in question lack the resources to fund independent Asian or Chinese studies centers. As some have noted, decisions taken within liberal democracies to censor prestigious journals at the source – or conversely to acquiesce implicitly to a highly sanitized, university-sanctioned version of China's story – gives the unfortunate impression to all that the CCP's version of history is the only one, endorsed by the international scholarly community.[ii]

This is particularly of concern in younger democracies, which frequently lack deep expertise on China. In regions of the world ranging from Latin America to Central Europe to sub-Saharan Africa, the Chinese government has actively shaped the "infrastructure of ideas" through backing think tanks, investing in media outlets and infrastructure, and co-opting elites through exchanges and privileged access to officials and experts in China. In this way, the CCP has restricted the diversity of knowledge and opinion on China in areas where it has strategic interests, with the most prominent and politically connected voices frequently being those associated with the CCP. Notably, this is not limited to positive advocacy for CCP objectives, but includes the marginalization or exclusion of issues that the CCP deems sensitive. This list of issues is constantly expanding, a dynamic that itself encourages even more self-censorship.

In the young and struggling democracies of sub-Saharan Africa, the Chinese government and government-linked companies have invested millions in communications infrastructure and media. Official Chinese cooperation arrangements with the continent – like the Forum on China-Africa Cooperation – have included arrangements for cooperation in film and TV production, Chinese support for radio and TV digitalization, and thousands of exchanges for African journalists. These "training" exchanges involve not so much training in the fundamentals of independent journalism but "training in the Chinese agenda," as some African independent journalists put it. The full ramifications of these developments have gone under-explored for a variety of reasons, including lack of capacity in the independent media sector to contextualize what is happening and clear incentives on the part of governments in Africa to cooperate with Chinese state objectives.

Finally, the Chinese government's multi-pronged effort to shape the future of the Internet has implications for free expression, privacy and surveillance globally. Chinese tech companies, now among the largest in the world, have pioneered domestic censorship and surveillance at home (in the absence of strong rule of law protections and civil society that can freely advocate for citizens' rights) while simultaneously pushing into overseas markets, a trend likely to accelerate under the Belt and Road Initiative. As I have noted elsewhere, it is reasonable to explore whether Chinese firms with global ambitions plan to follow the same CCP dictates with respect to data-gathering, surveillance and policing of communication abroad as they do at home. Meanwhile, the Chinese government continues to push its concept of "cyber sovereignty" at the international level, a model of authoritarian control over information that would end the Internet's potential to serve as a platform for global free expression. It is useful to note in this context that, rather than upholding values of free expression, Silicon Valley often invokes the "greater good" argument to justify censorship within the Chinese market.

The scale of these activities would have been impossible were it not for the tremendous market power China now wields. The CCP uses its unique carrots (including investments and market or other forms of access) in combination with its sticks (including denial of market and other forms of access, investment, or visas; and using pressure points on individuals and/or institutions) to create a foundation for its influence. As the Belt and Road Initiative rolls out throughout great swathes of the world, dwarfing the Marshall plan and engendering worries of "debt trap diplomacy," these carrots and sticks are likely to be deployed in greater measure.

<u>Addressing the challenge: prioritizing and reaffirming core democratic institutions and values</u>

Why is it important to address the "greater good" argument, advanced by those who say some degree of CCP-imposed censorship or interference is worth the trade-offs? Because in the eyes of the CCP, any decision by democracies to compromise their values is binary: either you are willing to do so or you aren't. Degree is unimportant. For some time, as the CCP's ambitions have grown, democracies have essentially conveyed the message that they are not willing to defend their own core values. As a result, the Chinese authorities increasingly set the rules with institutions within the democracies on standards of free expression, a development with enormously troubling implications if we remain on this trajectory.

Democracies are slowly coming to grips with this fact. Yet while the issue must be confronted head-on, it would be a mistake to think that the best way to address such heavy-handed tactics by authoritarian regimes is through similarly heavy-handed tactics by democracies that would have the effect of subverting the very values that undergird democratic systems. Democracies should be proactive in asserting why norms such as transparency, accountability, pluralism and the free exchange of ideas are critical to their interests. They must also be precise and thoughtful in formulating nuanced responses to authoritarian influence. Actions that fan xenophobia, restrict pluralism, or contravene core principles will not only weaken democratic institutions, but will conveniently make the CCP's own case that democracies are inherently flawed and hypocritical.

With this in mind, democracies might consider:

- Continuing to uncover the ways in which the CCP's influence activities are impinging on democratic institutions outside China's borders, and to share information on "best practices" for dealing with these activities while respecting democratic values;
- Facilitating democratic learning and supporting the capacity of local independent media to report in a dispassionate way on issues relating to China, particularly in countries or regions without deep capacity to do so;
- Seeking transparency in institutional agreements with Chinese government-affiliated institutions, such as Confucius Institutes and others. Particularly when public funds in democracies are involved, civil society should insist on understanding whether fundamental issues such as freedom of expression are placed at risk;
- Collectively supporting existing norms relating to academic freedom and freedom of expression (within publishing, the scholarly community, think tanks, etc.) so that individual actors are not as susceptible as they are now to being picked off and pressured by the Chinese government or its surrogates;
- Within relevant private sector industries, standing up initiatives that establish voluntary, mutual adherence to accepted norms of free expression and fundamental human rights;
- Encouraging democratic solidarity among countries that are grappling with their engagement with China. Such solidarity will invariably lead to more effective and democratically sustainable outcomes, given the scope of the challenge.

Thank you very much, and I look forward to answering your questions.

---

[i] *Sharp Power: Rising Authoritarian Influence*. International Forum for Democratic Studies, National Endowment for Democracy, December 2017. https://www.ned.org/wp-content/uploads/2017/12/Sharp-Power-Rising-Authoritarian-Influence-Full-Report.pdf Accessed 3/19/2018.

[ii] Alexander Dukalskis, "The Chinese Communist Party has growing sway in Western universities," Democratic Audit. http://www.democraticaudit.com/2018/01/04/the-chinese-communist-party-has-growing-sway-in-western-universities/ Accessed 3/19/2018.

Mr. YOHO. Thank you for your comments.
Dr. Kokas.

STATEMENT OF AYNNE KOKAS, PH.D., ASSISTANT PROFESSOR OF MEDIA STUDIES, UNIVERSITY OF VIRGINIA

Ms. KOKAS. Chairman Yoho, Ranking Member Sherman, and members of the U.S. House of Representatives Foreign Affairs Subcommittee on Asia and the Pacific, it is an honor to be here.

Funding from the FLAS, the Fulbright U.S. Student Program, the East-West Center, and the Woodrow Wilson Center where I am currently in residence have been central to my ability to research China both now and as a student in public universities in California and in Michigan.

Particularly in an era of increased Chinese influence in the United States, there is a crucial bipartisan national security need to fully fund the study of China by American scholars and students.

My remarks today focus on three key topics related to media industry influence—number one, the current challenges of Chinese influence on the U.S. media industries; number two, the challenges of deterring Chinese influence on the U.S. media industries; and number three, recommendations.

The regulatory landscapes of the Chinese and U.S. media industries differ starkly. While free market principles guide the U.S. media industry, Chinese media content is subject to highly centralized regulation.

Moreover, Chinese President Xi Jinping, as the chairman noted, has explicitly asserted the importance of expanding the favorable representation of China around the world through the media industries.

U.S. films face uncertainty in China's market. China and the U.S. are currently renegotiating the U.S.-China film agreement, which expired in February 2017, in response to the quota on foreign films imposed by this agreement.

Many U.S. studios participate in official Sino-U.S. film co-productions which circumvent the film quota in return for allowing Chinese regulators to shape content at every stage of the production process. And I am talking about big budget, $100 million—$200 million films.

Studios and other content producers also anticipate Chinese censorship. One Fox Television executive stated that their firm makes "China-compliant content" to reduce time to distribution for TV series with Chinese market aspirations, and these aren't TV series that have guaranteed distribution in China. These are just that aspire to Chinese distribution.

Now, Netflix has also discussed distributing "airplane cuts" or censored films in order to access the Chinese market.

The difficulty of accessing China's media market incentivizes U.S. firms to allow Chinese content standards to influence how they produce media for the global market.

Now, while U.S. firms face a highly restricted market entry environment in China, Chinese firms have a relatively free hand to invest in the United States.

Chinese firms have acquired U.S. studios like Legendary Entertainment, theatrical distribution infrastructure like AMC and Carmike, as well as establishing multi-film deals and individual film financing deals.

Now, under these circumstances the U.S. film industry has gone out of its way to collaborate with Chinese regulators.

In 2013, 2015, 2016, and 2017, U.S. media industry leaders invited Chinese regulators to give talks explaining how to comply with Chinese content regulations in Los Angeles.

Studios value the financial benefits of collaborating with Chinese partners in many ways more than they are concerned with the influence of Chinese regulators on content.

When the United States is no longer the largest media market in the world, which is rapidly approaching, U.S. leaders will have to decide what is more central: Financial growth or cultural influence.

And I realize that it's challenging to think about these things as a binary, but this is the situation that we may be in and we should at least consider.

Now, my recommendations are as follows. Based on research for my book, "Hollywood: Made in China," here are five recommendations to limit Chinese influence on the U.S. media industries.

Number one, prohibit Chinese regulators from lobbying U.S. industry leaders at events hosted in the United States.

Number two, require financial reporting of state-backed media production investment in the U.S. for any country the United States Trade Representative deems noncompliant with its WTO obligations for audio/visual industry.

Number three, consider a nonbinding resolution urging U.S. media producers to resist further censorship by foreign governments for the purposes of market entry, and this is part of a larger suite of activities which I think should occur in terms of raising awareness and calling out companies that are making statements suggesting that they're changing their content.

Number four, prohibit state-owned media investment in the U.S. by any country deemed by the United States Trade Representative to be noncompliant with WTO regulations for the audio/visual industry.

And number five, block U.S.-based IPOs for any media firms from countries that the USTR deems not to be in compliance with WTO market obligations.

Implementing these regulations will create a more difficult investment environment for state-backed Chinese firms seeking to influence Hollywood studios. It will also make it more inconvenient for Hollywood studios to make films shaped by Chinese regulators or backed by Chinese state-owned entities.

I would like to reiterate my gratitude to the U.S. Congress for its historical bipartisan support for the study of China and for giving me this opportunity to share my work.

Thank you.

[The prepared statement of Ms. Kokas follows:]

U.S. Responses to China's Influence Operations

Testimony of Aynne Kokas
Fellow, Kissinger Institute on China and the United States
The Woodrow Wilson Center for International Scholars
Assistant Professor of Media Studies, University of Virginia
House Foreign Affairs Committee
Subcommittee on Asia and the Pacific
March 21, 2018

Chairman Yoho, and distinguished members of the U.S. House of Representatives Foreign Affairs Committee Subcommittee on Asia and the Pacific, it is an honor to be here to discuss Chinese influence operations in the United States. I would first also like to take a moment to thank the US Congress for creating the conditions that have allowed me to testify here today. As a Greek-American educated in US public universities in Michigan and California, I would not have been able to learn Chinese or conduct research about China without funding from Title VI, the Fulbright US student program, the East-West Center, and the Woodrow Wilson Center, where I am currently in residence. Particularly in an era of increased Chinese influence in the United States, there is a crucial bipartisan national security need to fully fund the study of China by American scholars.

I will keep my remarks brief, focusing on three key topics:

1. The current environment of Chinese influence on the US media industries
2. The challenges of deterring Chinese influence on the US media industries
3. Recommendations

1. The current environment of Chinese influence on the US media industries

The United States' USD 13.3 billion positive trade surplus for the motion picture industry demonstrates the popularity of American films around the world. US citizens, permanent residents, and funding and talent from around the world have been instrumental in making Hollywood the global cultural juggernaut it is today. Indeed, Chinese talent in Hollywood has inspired box office blockbusters from *Crouching Tiger, Hidden Dragon* (Ang Lee, 2001) to many well-loved Jackie Chan films.

And yet, the regulatory landscapes of the Chinese and US media industries differ starkly. As Mike Ellis, Chairman of the Motion Picture Association, said in his address to the 2016 US-China Film Summit in Los Angeles, the US "market functions according to free market principles…in China according to a unique set of standards and guidelines." Ellis' comments elide the national-interest driven, highly centralized regulation of media content by Chinese government officials. More to the point, Chinese President Xi Jinping has explicitly asserted the importance of expanding the favorable representation of China around the world through the media industries.

Media industry oversight in China is only becoming tighter. On March 13, 2018, Patrick Frater reported in *Variety* that China's major state media regulator, formerly known as the State Administration of Press, Publication, Radio, Film, and Television (SAPPRFT), will be elevated to Cabinet-level oversight in the Chinese government. This reorganization of media regulation in China underscores the role that media plays in China's national-level political objectives.

US films face uncertainty in China's market. China and the United States are currently renegotiating the US-China Film Agreement, which expired in February 2017. The film agreement is most notable for its stated 34-film quota of revenue-sharing import films, which limits the number of foreign films that can be distributed in the market. Quota films must also pass Chinese censorship (formerly administered through SAPPRFT) after they are completed if they want to access the world's largest market.

One strategy US studios use to minimize market access risk is to participate in official Sino-US film co-productions. Film co-productions in the United States are based upon equity sharing. By contrast, in China, co-produced films must receive approval from the state-owned China Film Co-Production Corporation 1) before establishing the project; 2) during production; 3) after completion of the film. In return for allowing regulators to shape content, films that are successfully released as film co-productions both circumvent the film quota and receive a higher percentage of distribution revenue in the box office. Between the film quota and the co-production process, Chinese regulators have significant oversight over the production of films beyond the Chinese domestic market.

Another strategy that studios and other content producers use is to anticipate what Chinese regulators do and do not want to see, and tailor content accordingly. Ted Sarandos, the Chief Content Officer of Netflix, discussed distributing what he called "airplane cuts," or censored content, as a regulatory strategy for entering the Chinese market during a speech at the 2016 Consumer Electronics Show. Mike Ellis, the Chairman of the Motion Picture Association, based in Hong Kong, urged an audience of film producers at the 2016 US-China Film Summit in Los Angeles to be "aware of the sectors that you can do and those you need to avoid." One television executive at the 2015 US-China Film and Television Industry Expo in Los Angeles stated that their firm makes "China-compliant" content in order to reduce time to distribution for TV series with Chinese market aspirations. While these industry leaders rightly note that content has been tailored to local markets for a long time, the key piece that these industry discussions elide is that they are discussing not just cuts to media for specific markets after it is produced, but the process of conceptualizing and producing content for simultaneous distribution in global markets.

At the same time that firms in the United States are facing a highly restrictive market entry environment in China, Chinese firms have a relatively free hand to invest in the United States. Chinese firms have acquired US studios and theatrical distribution infrastructure, established multi-film deals and funded individual films. Only in the case of Dalian Wanda's spate of acquisitions in 2016 was there pushback against Chinese investment. In principle, Chinese investment in Hollywood is just another feature of a highly globalized media system. In practice, it occurs against the backdrop of an environment in which US firms have no reciprocal access to the Chinese market.

China's domestic media content control policies are under its domestic sovereignty. However, the United States Trade Representative stated in January 2018 that China is not meeting its World Trade Organization commitments with regard to its audiovisual market. The limitations China is placing on accessibility to its market create additional incentives for US firms to hew closely to Chinese content standards when they produce American films. China's domestic media policies, then, influence the behavior of US commercial firms.

2. The challenges of deterring Chinese influence on the US media industries

It is important to address trade issues such as WTO compliance and the renegotiation of China's film quota with the Chinese government during regular meetings. However, the political role of media in China makes it difficult to make headway in negotiations with the Chinese government. For this reason, it is perhaps even more important to address what happens in the United States and with US companies. Hollywood studios and other US-based global content producers are keenly aware of the rapid growth of the Chinese market. Indeed, they are dependent upon it for the continuous market growth expected of publicly traded companies.

Figure 1: Size of North American vs. Chinese Film Distribution Market Since 2011

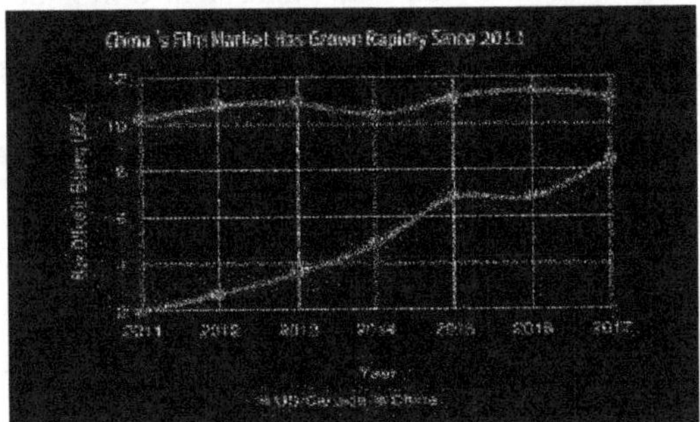

China already sells more movie tickets than the United States. Most estimates suggest that the Chinese film market will become the largest in the world within the next two years. Key Hollywood blockbusters are taking in more revenue in China than in the United States.

Figure 2: Selected 2017 Hollywood Blockbuster Box Office in the United States and China

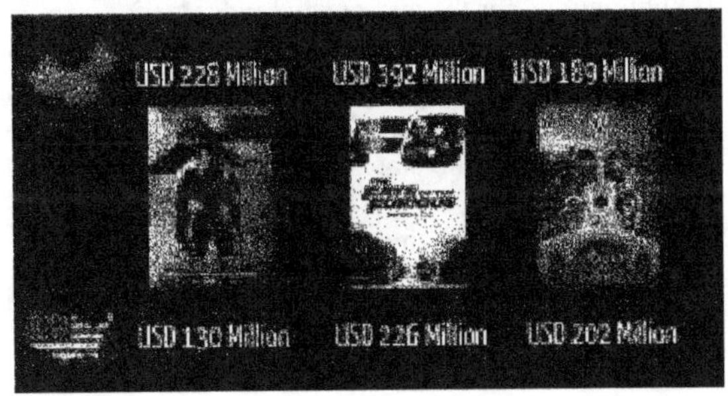

For the streaming market, China has more Internet users than the entire population of Europe. Thus, the key policy challenges that Congress faces are not merely related to Chinese government policies, but to the responses of US corporations to these policies.

The US film industry has gone out of its way to collaborate with Chinese regulators. In 2017, the head of the China Co-Production Corporation, a special organization authorized by the State Administration of Press, Publication, Radio, Film and Television, spoke to industry leaders at both the Asia Society US-China Film Summit and the US-China Film and Television Industry Expo (UCFTI) in Los Angeles about what type of content would be best suited to the Chinese market. In 2016, the Deputy Director of the State Administration of Press, Publication, Radio, Film, and Television addressed leaders at the UCFTI. In 2013, the General Manager of SAPPRFT spoke to the summit. All of these talks were given at the invitation of the conference organizers, who aimed to expand opportunities to access China's market.

As the actions of Hollywood leaders and industry forum organizers demonstrate, studios value the financial upside of collaborating with Chinese partners much more than they are concerned about the downside of having their work shaped by Chinese regulators. The interests of Hollywood studios in maximizing their profits have long aligned with the interests of the US government in expanding Hollywood's cultural influence around the world. The growth of China's media market challenges this paradigm. When the United States is no longer the most important media market in the world, US leaders will have to decide what is more central – financial growth or cultural influence.

3. Recommendations

I am proud to be the author of the book *Hollywood Made in China* (University of California Press, 2017), which formed the basis for many of the recommendations and the research that I share with you today. The book represents the culmination of five years of fieldwork in China and Los Angeles, including one year funded by a US student Fulbright grant. Below are six recommendations to limit Chinese influence on the US media industries:

- Prohibit Chinese government media regulators from lobbying US industry leaders at events hosted in the United States.
- Require financial reporting of state-backed media production investment in the US for any country the United States Trade Representative (USTR) deems non-compliant with its WTO obligations for the audiovisual industry.
- Consider a non-binding resolution urging US media producers to resist further censorship by foreign governments for the purposes of market entry.
- Continue progress on the expansion of CFIUS in media investment to include individual film productions, film slates, and partial acquisitions, but only with increased funding and increased expertise to ensure that the Committee is able to systematically review deals with the appropriate experts.
- Prohibit state-owned media investment in the US by any country deemed by the United States Trade Representative to be non-compliant with WTO obligations for the audiovisual industry.

- Block US IPOs by any media firms from countries that the USTR deems to be not in compliance with WTO audiovisual market obligations.

Implementing some or all of these recommendations will create a more difficult investment environment for state-backed Chinese firms seeking to influence Hollywood studios. They will have the effect of 1) making it more difficult for Chinese regulators and Chinese state-backed enterprises to operate in the US media industries; and 2) making it more inconvenient for Hollywood studios to make films shaped by Chinese regulators or backed by Chinese state-owned or state-influenced entities.

There is every indication that the influence of the Chinese state on the US media industries will continue to grow as the Chinese commercial market becomes a bigger, more lucrative target for Hollywood. Recent changes in the media regulatory apparatus in China also suggest that regulation of the Chinese commercial media market will tighten, further limiting the foreign content that will receive approval in China. However, it is of the utmost importance to remember that much of Hollywood's relationship with regulators in Beijing is a deliberately cultivated market entry strategy designed to access the world's largest media market.

In conclusion,

1. The market pressures on publicly traded US media conglomerates are driving them to allow Chinese regulators greater oversight over the media products they produce.

2. There are clear cultural and economic incentives to continue collaborations between non-state-owned Chinese firms and US media firms.

3. The United States media industries still have a higher global profile in production than the Chinese film industry and a wide range of potential capital investment from outside of China.

I would like to reiterate my gratitude to the US Congress for its historical bipartisan support for the study of China, and for giving me this opportunity to share my work. I look forward to taking your questions.

Mr. YOHO. Thank you for being here and we are excited about this because there's been a lot to talk about what China is doing and what their intent is, and I think it's very evident. It's right out in front of us if we just listen.

And, you know, I read your testimonies beforehand and I think you guys are all spot on and so we look forward to highlighting this so that we can make policies to direct what we do as a nation.

And I want to let you know how important it is that you're here because you're the ones that are giving us the expert advice and that a lot of times turns into recommendations we give to the State Department or to the administration and/or is legislation, as Mr. Wilson will talk about here in a minute.

But I think if we listen to just the words in the past, if we go back to Deng Xiaoping—well, actually if we go to Mao Zedong, in 1949 he mapped out a 100-year plan to rebuild the Chinese Empire, and he had the Great Leap Forward and he brought in all the laborers and they were going to feed all of China with the farm laborers.

It was forced labor. Production went down and millions of people died. During his reign, he's credited with 40 million to 80 million people dying under his reign.

But yet, they hail him as a great leader and a great philosopher. I don't know if we would do that in this country.

And then if you look at Deng Xiaoping, his quote, and again, this is building the direction of China. You know, you have got the 100-year mapped out under Mao Zedong—1949. We are well into that, almost 69 years into that, and then Deng Xiaoping quotes, "Hide our strength and bide our time," or another way is "Hide our capacities and bide our time."

And there was a great documentary that was done. I think it might have been in early 1980s when he said China cannot compete with Japan or other countries like the United States in computers and IT and manufacturing but what we can do is we can corner the market on rare earth metals, and they did.

And then you move on to Robert Gates' book, a book called "Duty." When we were negotiating military sales with Taiwan, as we've done since the 1970s, China always balked at it and didn't like it.

But in his book—I think it was in 2013 during the negotiations China raised holy Cain with their Ambassadors and their admirals saying how wrong this was and this was not right to do.

And our negotiator says, "Well, we've been doing this since the 1970s. Why now the complaint?" And this is what they said and I think, again, this is a signal—"Yes, I know you did. But back then, China was weak. We are strong now."

And then you move on to Xi Jinping and the 19th Party Congress back in October 2017 when he took center stage or he was up there, and he says that the era of China has arrived.

No longer will China be forced to swallow their interests around the world. The era of China has arrived for us to take the world's center stage.

I take that as a threat, you know, like they want to knock somebody off the stage, you know, and we shared this with people in Hong Kong in their pro-Beijing members that were there, and we said, I take that as a personal assault on Americans' sovereignty and that will not be tolerated and please carry that back to Beijing, and I hope they did.

And then with the opening statements here of what Xi Jinping just said—I guess it was this week—"We are resolved to fight the bloody battle against our enemies."

I think that's a concern for everybody—the bloody battles against our enemies. We are not at war with China. We are not at war with anything they're doing other than their aggression that they're showing in the South China Sea, their aggression against democracies around the world, and they're throwing out their form of socialism with Chinese characteristics, which I said in the opening statement, you can put lipstick on a pig, but it's still a pig.

You know, they can call it what they want but it's still communism because it's authoritarian rule. And you were so right talking about—actually it was Ms. Kalathil talking about the greater good argument of Silicon Valley, and Hollywood too, as you have brought up.

They're willing to sell the profits, they're willing to get rid of the integrity that makes a business great for the short-term profits. And, again, keep in mind China is playing the long game here and we need to smarten up. And I am thankful you're here to bring this out more in the open.

So how can we best counter what Xi Jinping's promotion of China's governance is and the model in the developing world? That's one.

Does this need to be done through diplomacy, trade, military, or all of the above? And is China using, in your opinion, the Belt Road initiative to drive countries toward this model?

And Mr. Mattis, if you will start and just answer these as quick as you can and we'll get on to the other members.

Mr. MATTIS. The first way, I think, to counter is that we have to do defense well.

It's not necessarily about what China is doing but protecting our own sovereignty because when we don't enforce our laws, when we don't protect our citizens, we are—and we don't protect our industries then we are ceding our sovereign rights as a government and as a country to allow this interference.

And all of these things start at home before they become questions of how do we deal with Chinese diplomacy—how do we deal with their efforts to expand their influence abroad?

Ms. KALATHIL. Thank you. With respect to the developing world and with other countries, one of the things that we found in our report on sharp power is that young democracies in particular who are interested in perhaps understanding more about China often don't have the capacity to do so.

Their independent media sectors are quite weak. They are easily susceptible to financial pressure or to being bought out by Chinese Government-related interests.

So there's a tremendous need to put China into context in these countries and in the countries that we studied which includes Slovakia, Poland, Argentina, and Peru. There are a number of other countries on the African continent where this would hold true as well.

So I think a first step, if we were to support or if democracies could support better understanding of China in a way that is not influenced by the Chinese Government's own narrative that would be a big step.

Mr. YOHO. Dr. Kokas.

Ms. KOKAS. I would like to reinforce what Mr. Mattis said regarding enforcing our own laws and institutions.

It's essential to set the standard and to identify what role we can play. But more importantly, I think within this context it's also important to continue to participate in multilateral and multi stakeholder regional institutions and I am particularly thinking about increased participation in multi stakeholder internet governance institutions where China has been making huge inroads and investing and sending staff to participate and set these new standards.

Thank you.

Mr. YOHO. Thank you.

Next, we'll go to Mr. Tom Marino.

Mr. MARINO. Thank you, Chairman.

I am going to approach this from a geopolitical position and then each of you can respond. I will start with you. I am sorry. I am drawing a blank on the name.

Ms. KOKAS. Kokas.

Mr. MARINO. Yes. We'll start with you, please.

Ms. KOKAS. All right.

Mr. MARINO. And then go to your right.

It is said that China will defeat the United States and other democracies not by its military. However, it will win by controlling the world market and international economy.

For example, take the continent of Africa and the countries within there. China takes oil and minerals, great abundances, and anything else it can get its hands on.

In return, China invests in Africa's infrastructure, finance, among other things and other ventures. This insincere philanthropy saddles Africa with large debt.

Nevertheless, this move by China is only the beginning. It is a test for China's growing international ambitions, i.e., in their sights Iran, Afghanistan, of course, North Korea, and South America.

Would you please comment on their aggression economically in these developing countries and continents?

Ms. KOKAS. Mr. Marino, thank you very much for that excellent question, and I think that one of the ways we need to frame this is how U.S. companies also operate within these spaces.

So when we are looking at financing and investment, U.S. companies have also been very active in investing in these markets and extractive industries.

Now, one of the key differences is the connection between the state, the party, and the industries, and this is the crucial distinction here.

Now, I think to the degree that Chinese investment is an extension of Chinese state power, this is concerning from my perspective in terms of setting standards, particularly setting standards for new industries and in developing countries that don't necessarily have those standards yet, particularly in telecommunications.

I think that this is also of concern when we are looking at potential industries such as rare earth where we have a larger long-term competition.

So thank you.

Ms. KALATHIL. Thank you.

You know, with respect to the countries of Africa and developing countries in general, I think China has made tremendous inroads not just with its investment but with its overall approach where it portrays itself as a fellow developing country that has actually managed to lift itself out of poverty very effectively, and I think it would be a mistake to discount the power of that narrative within developing countries because they do look to China as an example.

And so the narrative that China represents something of a model does not fall on deaf ears. I think it does have some resonance.

It is part of the challenge to be able to show the complexity of that rise and to show that there are aspects of the Chinese system of governance which may be inimical to democracies around the world.

This is not being clearly conveyed. I recently was in Africa talking to a number of independent journalists and civil society, activists, and there's a distinct dearth of knowledge with respect both to the Chinese internal system of governance as well as to the true ramifications of its investment and development policies overseas and, again, that goes back to a tremendous lack of capacity.

I think independent journalists have long tried to cover some of the aspects that Dr. Kokas just mentioned about the actions of multinationals in the mineral sector in developing countries and within Africa.

But there has been less attention to the Chinese presence and I think that's partly because the governments of many of these African countries have struck deals with the Chinese Government and it creates an environment that makes it very difficult to explore the true ramifications of those investments.

So these independent journalists and civil society activists and academics and policy makers throughout the developing world need the capacity to better understand the full ramifications of Chinese investments and to be able to report and discuss these things in a way that's free of Chinese Government influence.

Mr. MARINO. Thank you.

Mr. Mattis, you have 20 seconds.

Mr. MATTIS. We have the Foreign Corrupt Practices Act that can provide some effectiveness at dealing with practices that have clearly gone into the corrupt or the coercive.

We also have the ability to bring people to the United States and educate them. I will simply use the example of a friend of mine who is from Sudan or South Sudan and was brought to the U.S. and educated, and his brother did the same thing in China.

And their views of what governments should do, how they should act, how they should relate to civil society, how they should relate to media couldn't be starker.

Mr. YOHO. Thank you for the questions and the answers.

We'll next go to Mr. Connolly from Virginia.

Mr. CONNOLLY. Thank you, Mr. Chairman.

I don't know what you all did to scare up all the Democrats but I thought you'd want a little company.

At any rate, thank you, and thanks so much for being here.

Dr. Kokas, you come from, of course, one of the greatest universities on the planet. I lecture there once a year so I very much enjoy going down, and if you see Professor Gerry Warburg please say hello for me.

Ms. KOKAS. Absolutely.

Mr. CONNOLLY. He's a good friend at that school.

How worried should the United States be about the fact that China is exercising soft and sharp power, as it's been called, you know, and things like, you know, the new Silk Road, making enormous investments throughout the developing world, but they are fixed investments.

I mean, they're not moveable. They do indebt countries, and I was in Sri Lanka last year and in Hambantota they built a whole new port. They built a hospital.

They built the amphitheater and a conference center and all of it pretty empty, and the debt was beyond Sri Lanka's ability to carry it and, of course, now they're signing a long-term lease for the Chinese to manage it. It's in a strategic location that is of some concern to the United States and India.

But if they want to build stuff for other countries that is immovable, even if we think it's not a good economic investment or they could—there's an opportunity cost associated with this.

In a sense, how concerned are we to be?

Ms. KOKAS. So with a lot of the BRI investments, I am taking a wait and see approach because it will be interesting to see how developing countries respond to this over the long term because a lot of these deals are not great deals.

Now, I think that you make a great point that these are individual choices by individual sovereign countries and there's only a certain degree of influence that the U.S. can have in those situations.

I think what your point underscores is the need to participate in multi-stakeholder institutions and regional institutions very actively in order to be able to shape perspectives about these questions for people in these regions and for leaders in these regions.

But our ability to counteract Chinese investment in individual countries really can only be counteracted, from my perspective, by parallel investment or by influence in multi-stakeholder institutions.

So thank you.

Mr. CONNOLLY. Ms. Kalathil, what kind of good will is China aggregating to itself with these kinds of investments, especially when you hear and I've certainly heard in country after country they stick to themselves.

They create a Chinese camp. They don't hire local labor. They import Chinese labor. There's no ripple effect in the economy. Yeah, we are left with a new hotel or a hospital or whatever it is, but we haven't really reaped the benefits of local labor participating in the project and they're kind of aloof and separate and keep their own to themselves. They don't kind of mingle after hours with the locals.

You actually hear that in terms of certain—there's even a racial aspect to it. There's certainly an economic and social aspect to it.

How much good will do they muster from these kinds of investments, at the end of the day, do you think?

Ms. KALATHIL. Thank you. That is a good question.

I think one of the things that we discovered in putting together our sharp power report is that oftentimes with the Chinese Government it's less about fostering good will and perhaps rising numbers of people around the world who approve of China and it's more about achieving some kind of strategic interest, particularly when it comes to these kinds of investments.

You had mentioned the Belt Road initiative. You know, one under explored aspect of that is the digital Silk Road, which actually is less about fixed investment and more about transmission of media products, of various channels for influence.

Those sorts of things, again, are less about creating good will and less about accumulating some kind of positive image of China, more about conveying a very particular narrative about China and shutting down dissent around that.

Thank you.

Mr. CONNOLLY. Thank you, Mr. Chairman. My time is up.

Thank you all for being here.

Mr. YOHO. Thank you for your questions and answers.

Now we'll go to Mr. Rohrabacher from California.

Mr. ROHRABACHER. I know at times when you look at the public debate on what relations we should have with this country or that country, it is a bit disturbing for me to see not just double standards but triple standards when it comes to China, and that is China is investing in Hollywood movies today and taking about anything that China could be made to look bad.

That is incredible that we are letting another country do that to our communications in this country. "Independence Day"—that movie all of a sudden—major figures in the movie turned out to be Chinese generals and commanders, and just in the movie "Gravity"—I mean, it was based on an astronaut that went up and was being damaged by space debris and the original script it was a Chinese space station that exploded and caused the space debris.

But in the rewrite that the American people see, oh, it's—the Chinese are the heroes and she's saved by the Chinese space station.

Something's wrong there. Something's really wrong. We are allowing our people to have their minds molded in that way. This, quite frankly—I know I get a lot of criticism for making these comparisons—I mean, compared to what's going on with the Russians trying to influence our way of thinking, this is like 100 times beyond that.

I mean, they're hackers—we all know the hacking that goes on. In China massive hacking as compared to anybody else but it's way beyond anybody else in the world.

We are talking about the Third World countries, that now look to China as a developing country we could be like. They don't look at it that way.

The Chinese are bribing these people all up—all over the world and we aren't doing anything about it. We aren't stepping up to the plate, and they're bribing these people. The Third World dictators are selling out their own people in order to get short-term Chinese cash in their bank account somewhere in probably Switzerland or with an American and international financial communities as partners in this theft of Third World assets.

What are their assets? The poor people in these world they only have the assets of their country and that's being stolen from them by bribes from the—from not just Chinese businessmen.

Let me ask you this—is that bribery and that type of activity that I am talking about, is this just a bunch of Chinese businessmen operating independently of what their government wants or is this part of a strategy that the Chinese Government and the Chinese leadership have in order to achieve power and achieve their goals?

Maybe just go real quick down the line and I will let you comment on that.

Mr. MATTIS. I hate to give you a yes and no answer. But the Chinese Government does provide the direction and does not disapprove of the methods, I should say.

It's a goals-oriented approach to build relationships with foreign elites and if that requires bribes, if that requires an outrageous speaking fee to come speak at someone's resort, to think of John Ashe at the U.N. General Assembly, then they're willing to tolerate those kinds of methods or to encourage them where that's appropriate.

Ms. KALATHIL. I would agree with Peter Mattis' comments and also add that I think that the Chinese Government is also quite aware of those institutions in developing countries as well as democracies that may appreciate the money.

And sometimes this is not in the form of bribery. It comes in other forms and I think that's what we have to try and shine a light upon.

But we also have to understand that in the case of, for instance, educational institutions it's a very tricky issue because if the Chinese Government comes with money and says, we'd like to fund some sort of initiative to study China but it has to be according to certain specifications, it's very difficult for institutions that are strapped for money to say no to that and I think that's the added dimension of that.

Mr. ROHRABACHER. Let's hope so because we see this Chinese money actually influencing different people as to whether we will permit certain people to march in a parade in our own country.

We've seen that. We've seen a hostile country that's government is hostile to things we believe in, preventing people—the Falun Gong and others—from marching in parades in our country.

That's outrageous. But I don't see much focus on it.

Ms. KOKAS. Thank you very much for the question.

This is outside of my area of expertise so I yield my time.

Mr. ROHRABACHER. All right. Well, thank you very much, Mr. Chairman.

Mr. YOHO. Thank you for bringing that out.

Next we'll go to Mr. Joe Wilson, who is the author of the Foreign Influence Transparency Act, I believe it is.

Mr. WILSON. Yes.

43

Mr. Yoho. Thank you.

Mr. Wilson. And thank you, Chairman Ted Yoho, for your vision to conduct this hearing on foreign influence today.

I appreciate the witnesses for taking time to address the growing concern of Chinese influence in our democracy. As a grateful son of a World War II Flying Tiger who served in China where he developed a great fondness for the people of China, I value working together with China for mutual benefit of our countries.

However, it is troubling when China takes advantage of this relationship. One issue in particular that I have been working on is China's ongoing influence campaign through the establishment of its Confucius Institutes throughout the United States, which I appreciate Chairman Ted Yoho citing earlier today.

There are currently 103 active Confucius Institutes that were described in 2009 by Lin Chang Chung, the head of propaganda for the Chinese Communist Party, "As an important part of China's overseas propaganda set-up."

It is for this reason that yesterday I introduced H.R. 5336, the Foreign Influence Transparency Act, which would require transparency of these institutes and institutes like that through modifying the Foreign Agent Registration Act to promote public disclosure.

And for each witness, do you believe it's appropriate to require organizations like the Confucius Institutes to register under the Foreign Agent Registration Act?

And we'll begin with Dr. Kokas. I attended JAG school at UVA so I have a fondness for your institution.

Ms. Kokas. We always love meeting our alums and especially ones doing such wonderful things.

Mr. Wilson. Thank you.

Ms. Kokas. So thank you so much for that great question, and as a professor this is a particularly meaningful issue for me, and what I would underscore is there is a very easy way to get Confucius Institutes off of U.S. campuses and that is by increasing the funding for the study of Chinese from the U.S. Federal Government.

And for my colleagues and my students who are using these resources, most of it has to do with a lack of state and Federal funding for the study of the Chinese language.

So this isn't because we are preferenced to bring Chinese faculty onto campuses or into elementary schools or middle schools or high schools. It's because at the state, local, and national level, Chinese language education has been severely cut.

Now, to your question about whether or not it's valuable to register Confucius Institutes under FARA, I am hesitant to support that approach because of the importance of academic freedom and I do question how this type of registration would not only affect things domestically but also for U.S. students and scholars who are trying to go abroad and study abroad in China.

And I think, as you pointed out, continuing this dialogue and continuing to be able to have scholarly and academic exchange is essential for future development and growth of the relationships between our two countries.

Mr. WILSON. And, of course, what I am proposing is not a bar at all.

Ms. KOKAS. Yes.

Mr. WILSON. It's disclosure and for students to know——

Ms. KOKAS. Yes.

Mr. WILSON [continuing]. The relationship with the government, with the Communist Party and not at all a bar to Mandarin language or whatever.

Ms. KOKAS. Yes. So I think that there definitely is an upside to identifying more clearly what those origins are and I will tell you a story about something when I was in Virginia.

I was giving a talk at William and Mary, and there was a Confucius Institute leader who oversaw a talk that I was giving and asked specific leading conversations, and I didn't know before I went to give the talk that the Confucius Institute was sponsoring the talk.

So there are a lot of different ways in which this can have influence and that actually shaped our discussion in the talk and the ways in which I had to, as a professor, respond to a lot of these issues.

So I think that that is important. But I think one of the best ways to counteract that, again, is increased funding for Chinese language education.

Thank you.

Mr. WILSON. Thank you.

Ms. KALATHIL. Thank you, Representative Wilson.

While I can't speak to the specifics of your proposed legislation, I would say that I think democracies in general would appreciate and do well from increased transparency around Confucius Institutes.

I think that also happens at the institutional level and what we found is that much of the knowledge about Confucius Institutes comes from reporting and in the United States from FOIA, and there has to be a better way to increase transparency around the agreements that universities have struck with the Confucius Institutes and a way to get that information out to the broader public.

Mr. WILSON. Thank you very much.

Mr. Mattis.

Mr. MATTIS. I am firmly in favor of the discussion that your bill creates because it is about a conversation about what is appropriate—what are the rules of engagement.

The agreements should be open and they should be important. I think Confucius Institutes are not important for the individuals that are in them that are brought over from China as language teachers or whatever else.

They're important for the institutional relationship that is established between the university and Hanban back in China or ultimately the United Front Work Department and it's that that institutional relationship provides leverage.

So it's less about the individuals that are there and more about how that connection or how the loss of funding or how the loss of other academic programs might be used to pressure those universities.

Mr. WILSON. And I thank each of you and thank you again, Chairman Yoho.

Mr. YOHO. Thank you.

We'll next go to Mr. Chabot of Ohio.

Mr. CHABOT. Thank you, Mr. Chairman.

First of all, I apologize for coming a little late. As you probably maybe already announced, there were two Foreign Affairs hearings going on at the same time.

The other was on Saudi Arabia potential nuclearization and things right across the hall and so I went there and now here. So if I am repeating anything, I apologize, and I will just kind of throw this open and—and this to anybody.

First of all, as far as pressure, censorship, et cetera, either from the Chinese Government or Chinese interests either at home or especially here in the U.S. on a couple of groups that I just wanted to ask you about, first, just on, you know, students and making sure that the Chinese side of things kind of pushes out everything else—that they get their message through and the pressure that they're putting on entities here in the U.S.

Anybody want to talk about that? I know you have already talked about this to some degree but I will open it up.

Yes, sir.

Mr. MATTIS. So you're asking about sort of the nature of what Chinese students here in the United States are subjected to from their own government?

Mr. CHABOT. Correct.

Mr. MATTIS. Well——

Mr. CHABOT. And also perhaps former citizens of China who now have either become U.S. citizens or still have family members back there who they have to keep in mind that they may be under pressures or threats back home even though they happen to be here now.

Mr. MATTIS. First, they get used as props for rallies and attendees at sort of where Chinese leaders are present in—as a counter protest, for example, during the Olympic torch relays in 2008—to put pressure on representatives who have large Chinese constituencies that can be used to promote letter-writing campaigns or email-writing campaigns about Tibet, about human rights, about other policy or suggestions that are antithetical to the Party.

Second, there is, in some cases, very direct coercion put on family members and someone who has done something in the United States, to pick, for example, the Radio Free Asia reporters who have been reporting on the crackdown in Zheijiang were contacted and told that they had family members who had been arrested and that if they were to be released that they would need to stop their reporting.

And these kinds of threats are more common than we know in part because there's no real safe place for people to turn to say, this is what's happening to me, this is what is occurring.

And so, in a sense, we are allowing a foreign government to commit acts of violence, intimidation, to violate the civil rights of our own citizens or people who are protected by our law on our soil.

Mr. CHABOT. Thank you.

Another group that was particularly targeted in the PRC was Falun Gong, obviously, and I've read several books that came out within the last few years about literally members that were swept up over there and put in hospitals and literally organs harvested.

And, you know, it sounds so over the top that one might think that this is just kind of made up. But everything that I've seen it's absolutely true and we've had quite a few Falun Gong practitioners that I met with in my office and we've had in committees here over the years and they also have talked about, you know, family members back home that the government in their various ways keep an eye on them over here and there's retribution back there, whether or not they're practitioners in the PRC or not.

So anybody want to touch on Falun Gong you may not already have prior to me getting here? Yes.

Ms. KALATHIL. I mean, I can just briefly say that I think your identifying this issue is something that is happening within China as well as outside of China is quite pertinent and that extends not only to the Falun Gong but all these other groups that the Chinese Government considers sensitive, whether it's members of the Tibetan exile community or students that support more exploration of that idea.

That is what is the most concerning, and I would just add in addition to what Peter said about the coercions of Chinese students in the United States, which I think is absolutely correct, and I think that the emphasis actually is correct on the Chinese Government for exerting that pressure.

One gap that seems to have been identified is that those students are particularly vulnerable because they lack the broader bridges to the community and the university and so it is perhaps incumbent upon universities to try to create a better atmosphere so that those students also feel more connected to the university and they're not so dependent on the consulates for support and guidance.

Ms. KOKAS. Could I add——

Mr. CHABOT. Yes, ma'am.

Ms. KOKAS [continuing]. Very briefly to that?

Yes, and in the university environment there is a challenge, because a lot of Chinese students exist within Chinese language communities in which bullying or coercion occurs over Chinese social media, and then even when the students take it to the university administration it's difficult for the university to actually act upon it because there isn't enough support for international institutes and international studies at the institution for there to be Chinese language-speaking administrators who can help to address these challenges.

So there are actually mechanisms in place at the university level to help support and protect students that are being bullied by other students.

But the challenge of our multinational and global universities is that there frequently isn't enough support for international students. So I would just urge additional support of that nature.

Mr. CHABOT. Thank you very much.

My time has expired, Mr. Chairman.

Mr. YOHO. Thank you for your questions. Thank you for your great answers.

If you have got just a little bit more time I would like to ask a couple other things and Ranking Member Sherman may be back here. He had to vote.

Actually, we've got Scott Perry here. Are you ready to go—ask questions or do you want me to talk for a minute?

All right. Go ahead. I will yield to you right now.

Mr. Scott Perry from Pennsylvania.

Mr. PERRY. Thank you, Mr. Chairman. I am sorry to be late here. There's too many things going on.

But I will just do some blanket stuff and we'll see who wants to answer the questions. I am concerned about the Confucius Institute and their operations in the United States, the amount of students that they have studying here. The fealty that is paid by the universities, so to speak, to China because they fund their students here and, of course, the universities want that funding.

They pay the full ride and many American students can't afford to come to the schools. So not only is it that influence that comes from the students being here and taking information back to China, which might be otherwise proprietary or just as soon proprietary, but also from the teaching component of Chinese professors that are propagandizing.

And so, in a sense, I don't know what the vehicle is but I would be interested to hear from you folks what you think we can do about that from the standpoint of we have an open society with a First Amendment, right.

But that doesn't mean that we wish for other hostile nations or adversarial nations to come in and utilize the provisions of our constitutional freedoms to undermine our Government and our society. But, literally, I don't think there's any question really that that's happening.

So the question for you is what do we do in the confines of the constitutionality and current law to address that, and if we don't have current law to address it, what would you propose would be appropriate?

Ms. KOKAS. Mr. Perry, may I take that question?

Mr. PERRY. Please do.

Ms. KOKAS. Thank you very much, and thank you for that excellent question.

And I would actually like to tell you a personal story that relates directly back to this. So my graduate funding was supported by FLAS—Foreign Language Area Studies—and through that funding I actually taught Mandarin to two students, both Chinese students and U.S. students, at University of California, Los Angeles.

The gutting of that program means that my current institution where I teach—the University of Virginia—does not have that type of funding anymore.

So that's graduate students who aren't being funded. That's fewer Chinese language classrooms that are being offered. These are not expensive programs.

When we think about the potential possibility for countering Chinese influence, using already existing programs that are already in place, adding additional funding there, and allowing universities that don't necessarily have funding to teach Chinese language to use U.S. Federal Government funding rather than Confucius Institutes.

Most of the institutions that rely on Confucius Institutes to teach Chinese language are not doing so because they prefer to take money from Hanban.

It's because they don't have any other options and they believe that it's important to train their students for the 21st century.

Mr. PERRY. And I agree with that——

Ms. KOKAS. Yes.

Mr. PERRY [continuing]. And I agree with you that that's important and that is one of the benefits, right. It's great to have that other language and if the Chinese Government wants to pay for us——

Ms. KOKAS. Yes.

Mr. PERRY [continuing]. To have our students learn it, I am all for that.

The question is the propaganda that comes along with maybe not the language teaching——

Ms. KOKAS. Yes.

Mr. PERRY [continuing]. But the other components.

Ms. KOKAS. So I can give you actually some very specific recommendations with regard to this.

First of all, there are other foreign governments that pay for language and cultural education. So, for example, the Korea Foundation pays for professors and endows professorships.

However, the institution is able to select who the professor is. This is a crucial difference. So the professors and the teachers of Chinese language at universities and elementary schools and middle schools and high schools are selected by the Chinese Government.

So working with deals in order to be able to only accept that funding provided that that institution has more oversight over who was actually selected as the professor is one important——

Mr. PERRY. So can I ask you something about that?

Ms. KOKAS. Yes.

Mr. PERRY. How has that been determined? Is that a country by country proviso or is that just kind of the way it's done—China demands to have this selection right as a component or proponent of the funding coming along with it, and if the schools, for instance, says no, we reserve the right to choose the instructor then China just says no, is that because there's nothing in law.

There's nothing in statute or rule or whatever that is a prohibition. It's just a country by country agreement with school by school.

Ms. KOKAS. Precisely. Yes.

The other point that's important to note is that one thing that's quite easy to do is actually put up and create more transparency in the MOUs that different universities are signing because different universities sign different agreements with Confucius Institutes and typically institutions that have less institutional power and less finding sign less favorable agreements.

So a database of MOUs. Also, the ability the requirement that all institutions be able to leave that Confucius relationship on the spot if there are any perceived violations is also an important point.

Mr. PERRY. Are there privacy concerns if, assuming that most of the institutions that accept Confucius Institute funding and also Federal funding at the same time, are there privacy concerns from the institution's standpoint that they would not want to make those agreements open to public scrutiny or government scrutiny?

Ms. KOKAS. That's beyond my expertise.

However, my guess would be in a public institution there would be more flexibility than in a private institution with regard to those agreements.

Mr. PERRY. I yield, Mr. Chairman.

Ms. KOKAS. Thank you.

Mr. YOHO. No, I appreciate your dialogue and you bring up a very important issue. You know, you're talking about our former government and open—you know, all of our amendments but freedom of speech, freedom to participate, and I think it's time for us as a nation we need to look at these things when we have foreign countries, as we've seen with Russia, as we've seen with China, dictating or pushing the narrative that weakens our democracy and bolsters their—and, you know, the last thing that China wants is a successful democracy and we see them going after Cambodia.

We see them going after all these fledgling democracies and their wish is that they fall apart so that they can have the Socialist form of government that they proclaim with Chinese characteristics, as you and I know as communism, and they want to promote that.

So I think this is a dialogue maybe we need to continue and I appreciate you bringing that up.

If you have time, and I think the best way to phrase this is I want to start out with the United Front, which is a soft power advocate for China, and the role of the Chinese—they said in this the role of the Chinese citizen is to serve the Communist Party and that's the antithesis of what we believe here in America.

You know, we believe our rights come from a Creator and that government is instituted by we the people to protect our God-given rights and that the government is there to fight for the protection of your rights, not to serve government.

And so we are at polar opposites and I would like to see how that plays out in their future. I kind of see how it will.

I want to ask you, with the statements I made in the beginning about the different sayings by the different leaders and knowing what China is doing, they're wiping out past cultures while rewriting their own history.

If you look at Tibet, they're changing the demographics of the Tibetan region and putting in Chinese nationals to dilute the population, eventually, getting rid of the Tibetan history.

They're doing this with Mongolia. Certainly they're doing it with Hong Kong. You know, that used to be part of Great Britain and they let it go back in I think it was 1997. But with Taiwan it's a different story.

You know, Taiwan fought a civil war. They lost. They moved to Taiwan, and it was recognized as a country until the Nixon era.

But, again, China is stepping in and has made bloody threats over these countries. But my question to you, when it comes to businesses in America are there pure Chinese nationals—just Chinese citizens that have come here but they're still Chinese citizens that have created businesses in the U.S. without the influence or the hand of the CCP—the Chinese Communist Party—in your experience or in your research?

Mr. Mattis, go ahead. You look like you want a bite at that.

Mr. MATTIS. Well, I would say that here are plenty of examples of Chinese citizens who have come to the United States for the same reason that many predecessors from Europe, from Africa, from elsewhere in the world has come to the United States—that this is a place where there is opportunity. This is a good place to be an entrepreneur.

This is a good place to raise a family. And so there are definitely examples of people who have come for all of the reasons that we recognize and celebrate.

Mr. YOHO. Okay. But if we go up to a bigger scale business, say, that employs 100 or 500 people, would it change? Would they be here on their own or would they—you know, we know the people that have restaurants and, you know, small businesses.

But as you get to a larger business would that hold true for that or would you see a hand of the Chinese Government—their Secret Service or military?

Mr. MATTIS. That depends on their interests back in China.

Mr. YOHO. Okay.

Mr. MATTIS. If they have substantial business interest there, then they are vulnerable to coercion. They could be punished for participating in political activities that the Party doesn't want through the—sort of the compromise of their assets back home.

Mr. YOHO. Okay.

Ms. Kalathil, any comments, or Dr. Kokas, either one?

Ms. KALATHIL. I think just to add to Peter's comments, you know, I think at the level of the larger companies within that are vulnerable to CCP influence, I would say it's more relevant to those companies that have started within China and that are now moving overseas as opposed to the situation that you described.

I think you can find many, many companies that were started in China in the absence of significant foreign competition perhaps and that now are moving overseas and through a variety of means of influence the Party is able to pull levers over what they invest in or how they direct their interests.

Ms. KOKAS. So to build on what Shanthi and Peter had mentioned, my major concern in this case is actually that by not supporting immigrant entrepreneurs that rather than staying in the United States and building technology here that they decide to return to China because this is no longer a hospitable place.

And I will give an example of an AI company that I was speaking at a conference that I was at at Brown that was developing mobility technology as well as new medical technologies and the founder was trained in the Bay Area at public institution, worked at Google, and then because of discrimination that he and his family felt, he went back to China and established his company there.

So my major concern is actually in that way, that we lose out on incredible immigrant talent because of any kind of——

Mr. YOHO. All right. Was he a Chinese national?

Ms. KOKAS. He was a Chinese national.

Mr. YOHO. Okay. And remember what we said in the beginning. China will come out and say this is a form of racism. So, you know, I don't want to have conspiracies going on. But——

Ms. KOKAS. But this wasn't a Chinese Government official that was saying this. This was——

Mr. YOHO. Right.

Ms. KOKAS [continuing]. The individual that was saying it in a personal conversation.

Mr. YOHO. But we know first hand that there's students going to MIT that have already gotten their graduate degree in China.

Then they've come over here to apply as a brand new student and they get accepted to the better programs because of their talent, and we know this first hand.

I've just seen too many examples and the reason I brought up the first question about the purity of a Chinese business is because I've had so many business people that say if a Chinese business is here, just assume it's their government, their Secret Service, and military because it's all one. They're all connected.

You know, the role of the Chinese people is to serve the government and if they're a Chinese national—this is what I've been told—and we've had one of our agencies—three-letter agencies that I can't talk about, and he just said if you're on the internet just assume China's in your internet. I mean, we know these things, and so I think we need to tread a little bit smarter.

You had another comment you wanted to say.

Ms. KOKAS. Yes. Of course. Thank you very much, Chairman Yoho.

With all due respect, once we start conflating Chinese people in the United States with the Chinese Government, then we risk moving back to very, very dark periods of our nation's history.

Mr. YOHO. I think that's fair. I think that's real fair and that's something we really need to watch for.

But on the same token, we can't be naive with what, like Mr. Perry brought up that we have an open society. We operate on these rules and other people don't, to their advantage.

Mr. Perry, do you have any other comments you want to make?

Mr. PERRY. I don't think the chairman is talking about is Chinese people living in the United States. I think what he's talking about is the Chinese Government that sponsors either students, professors, or business people with the express purpose of coming to the United States to parlay either what they get here or what they can do here for the good of the Chinese Government, and certainly that's not Chinese people that are in the United States that love America and want to be an American and live the American dream and have that opportunity.

But I think I would agree with the chairman that we would be naive as a country and as individuals to think that China has the United States' best interest at heart.

They want access to our markets but they would certainly rather not see us be a society that has free markets and open competition.

They prefer the Socialist/Communist model and they have since the 1950s and the 1940s when they changed to that model and they have shown no proclivity whatsoever to change that at all.

So I think we just have to be clear-eyed about the reality of the circumstance and do what we have to do within the confines of our Constitution to preserve our free democracy.

And if we don't, we don't do that at our own peril.

Mr. YOHO. And I think that's a good point being brought up because, you know, you look at our country and we've got so many great diasporas here, whether it's the Korean, the Vietnamese. You know, they've assimilated and become proud Americans with their heritage and we all accept that.

But I think in what's going on there's a different China than there was before. We've never seen the threat to democracy in my life. I will be 63 next month. I expect a birthday card from you.

But I've never seen this in my lifetime. You know, I grew up during the Nikita Khrushchev era and I remember him knocking on the podium with his shoe. But that was different.

You know, what we are seeing now is the subversive and the aggressive power of China, and we didn't even get into the South China Sea.

You know, if we look back at 2000, there was less than 50,000 Chinese students in here. Today, there's over 329,000.

Keeping in mind what Deng Xiaoping said or Mao Zedong said in 1949, they have a 100-year plan. You can fall into the conspiracy and you can get wrapped up in that or you can be cautious and move cautiously and I think that's what we are looking to do out of this hearing is how do we form policies.

And you brought up a great point—we can't be xenophobic about anybody but we sure need to be cautious about how we tread and we need to value who we are as a nation so that it stays there for another 100 years from now.

And, you know, we look at what's going on in Australia—the bribing of a senator to be favorable to Chinese policies. We know that's happened. We know they got caught.

It's the ones that didn't get caught that we don't know about— could that be in our country? These are things we always need to watch and the Australian national who went back to China to bury his father's ashes with his mother and they stopped him, and it was a message to send to other Chinese nationals that your political views are not welcome here so that it's a form of suppression for other people.

You know, I can't tell you much I thank you. Our team back here has already told us they've got a couple ideas for bills. So thank you, and we appreciate your time.

The committee, the Subcommittee on the Asia-Pacific, Foreign Affairs, as of this date, March 21st, has come to an end, sadly.

But we appreciate it, and it's adjourned. Thank you for your time.

[Whereupon, at 3:26 p.m., the committee was adjourned.]

APPENDIX

Material Submitted for the Record

SUBCOMMITTEE HEARING NOTICE
COMMITTEE ON FOREIGN AFFAIRS
U.S. HOUSE OF REPRESENTATIVES
WASHINGTON, DC 20515-6128

Subcommittee on Asia and the Pacific
Ted Yoho (R-FL), Chairman

March 14, 2018

TO: MEMBERS OF THE COMMITTEE ON FOREIGN AFFAIRS

You are respectfully requested to attend an OPEN hearing of the Committee on Foreign Affairs, to be held by the Subcommittee on Asia and the Pacific in **Room 2167** of the Rayburn House Office Building (and available live on the Committee website at http://www.ForeignAffairs.house.gov):

DATE: Wednesday, March 21, 2018

TIME: 2:00 p.m.

SUBJECT: U.S. Responses to China's Foreign Influence Operations

WITNESSES: Mr. Peter Mattis
                   Fellow
                   China Program
                   The Jamestown Foundation

                   Ms. Shanthi Kalathil
                   Director
                   International Forum for Democratic Studies
                   National Endowment for Democracy

                   Aynne Kokas, Ph.D.
                   Assistant Professor of Media Studies
                   University of Virginia

By Direction of the Chairman

COMMITTEE ON FOREIGN AFFAIRS

MINUTES OF SUBCOMMITTEE ON _______________ *Asia and the Pacific* _______________ HEARING

Day __*Wednesday*__ Date ______*March 21*______ Room ______*2167*______

Starting Time ___*2:00 pm*___ Ending Time ___*3:26 pm*___

Recesses |____| (____to ____) (____to ____) (____to ____) (____to ____) (____to ____) (____to ____)

Presiding Member(s)

Chairman Ted Yoho

Check all of the following that apply:

Open Session ☑
Executive (closed) Session ☐
Televised ☐

Electronically Recorded (taped) ☐
Stenographic Record ☐

TITLE OF HEARING:

U.S. Responses to China's Foreign Influence Operations

SUBCOMMITTEE MEMBERS PRESENT:

Yoho, Marino, Rohrabacher, Chabot, Perry
Sherman, Titus, Connolly

NON-SUBCOMMITTEE MEMBERS PRESENT: *(Mark with an * if they are not members of full committee.)*

Francis Rooney, Joe Wilson

HEARING WITNESSES: Same as meeting notice attached? Yes ☑ No ☐
(If "no", please list below and include title, agency, department, or organization.)

STATEMENTS FOR THE RECORD: *(List any statements submitted for the record.)*

SFR- Connolly

TIME SCHEDULED TO RECONVENE __________
or
TIME ADJOURNED ______*3:26*______

Subcommittee Staff Associate

Statement for the Record
Congressman Gerry Connolly
AP Subcommittee Hearing: "U.S. Responses to China's Foreign Influence Operations"
March 21, 2018

The Chinese Communist Party (CCP) has pursued a range of policies to tighten its grip on power at home and expand its influence abroad. As Xi Jinping recommits China to the path of authoritarianism by abolishing presidential term limits, he is using similar authoritarian tactics – specifically state-directed and funded propaganda – to conduct foreign influence operations in the United States and other countries. As adversaries like China and Russia advance covert efforts to exert influence on U.S. domestic and foreign policy, we must respond by strengthening our democratic institutions and reinforcing our defenses against foreign interference.

The National Endowment for Democracy coined the term "sharp power" to describe the aggregate impact of foreign influence operations directed by Chinese and Russian authoritarian regimes. China's interference is carried out through a variety of mediums, including the media, academia, politics, and public discourse. Some of the most prominent sources of China's interference are the Confucius Institutes, which are Chinese government-funded educational centers that tend to operate in partnership with academic institutions. While these institutes often provide funding and educational opportunities, they also peddle Chinese propaganda and threaten freedom of expression by pressuring teachers to engage in censorship. The National Association of Scholars has recommended that all universities close any related Confucius Institutes and called for legislative action to address them.

According to a March 2018 Gallup poll, 53 percent of Americans have a favorable opinion of China, a higher percentage than at any other point since the 1989 Tiananmen Square massacre. Given that Beijing continues to undertake actions that threaten U.S. economic and national security interests, China's high favorability among Americans underscores how perception is not in line with reality. Beijing's state-directed cyberattacks, noncompetitive trade practices, intellectual property theft, and lack of cooperation on the North Korean nuclear threat should give the American people plenty of reasons to view China with great skepticism.

The United States cannot allow foreign powers to attack covertly democratic principles and whitewash their own authoritarian regimes. We must engage in democracy promotion at home and abroad, insist on transparency for foreign-directed influence campaigns, and shutdown illegal influence operations that undermine American democratic institutions. Propaganda funded by foreign powers is not the free press and should not expect treatment as such. The health of our democracy depends on a robust response to such foreign illegitimate interference. I look forward to hearing from our witnesses regarding how Congress can effectively prevent and counter China's "sharp power" while bolstering democratic resiliency in the United States and our partner countries around the world.

www.ingramcontent.com/pod-product-compliance
Lightning Source LLC
Chambersburg PA
CBHW080042260726
48658CB00007B/2704